The Big Tech Score

THE
BIG
TECH
SCORE

A Top Wall Street Analyst Reveals Ten Secrets to Investing Success

MIKE KWATINETZ
DANIELLE KWATINETZ WOOD

John Wiley & Sons, Inc.

New York • Chichester • Weinheim • Brisbane • Singapore • Toronto

ISBN 0-471-39592-7

Printed in the United States of America.

10 9 8 7 6 5 4 3 2 1

Contents

- Summing Up
- Interview with Larry Solomon, Capital Group

CHAPTER 7 87

Love Companies Customers Love

- Providing Better Service
- Creating an Elite Product
- Delivering More Value
- Putting It Together
- Summing Up
- Interview with Fred Kobrick, Kobrick Capital Fund

CHAPTER 8 105

Look for Long-Term Thinkers

- Prime Examples of Short-Term Thinking
- Going Long
- Prime Examples of Long-Term Thinking
- Summing Up
- Interview with Roger McNamee, Integral Capital Partners

CHAPTER 9 117

Always Look Forward, Not Backward

- Betting on the Old-Timers
- Betting on the New Wunderkind
- The Do-It-Yourself Mentality
- Summing Up

CHAPTER 10 137

Pick Only High-Growth Companies

- What Spurs Growth?
- The Stockholder Screen Test
- Growth Is Hard to Maintain
- Summing Up

Foreword

There are people that each of us meet over the course of our lives who are truly extraordinary at what they do. Such a person might be a doctor, an architect, or a teacher you had in high school. They come from all walks of life. While you're not always exactly sure what it is that makes them extraordinary, you recognize it when you see it. You don't need to spend even five minutes with John Chambers, of Cisco, to realize: Hey, this guy isn't just good, he's spectacular. I put Mike Kwatinetz in that upper echelon of extraordinary people.

I met Mike in 1991. I don't actually remember what stock we first talked about. Mike was an analyst at Sanford Bernstein and I was immediately impressed with the depth of his knowledge. Before becoming an analyst, Mike was a mathematician and a software engineer. It was apparent from our first meeting that he had a true first-hand sense of the software industry and the complexities inherent in technology investing.

We have talked about dozens of companies over the years, as well as the whole technology landscape—Microsoft, Dell, Cisco, the recent rise in the popularity of Linux, Sun Microsystems, the fragmentation of Unix, IBM, Apple, and many more. With respect to Microsoft and Dell, two positions in which we both made a lot of money for our clients and shareholders, we debated everything— from various new products to their respective Internet strategies, the direct-sales model to the various lawsuits (there were actually three), and the proliferation of NT to what the future holds for each company. Mike had an uncanny ability to identify the key variables early on and the conviction to stay focused on the fundamentals.

I am not the only person who feels this way. From time to time, I've talked with managers from around the country. It's very clear that my contemporaries feel the same way as I do about Mike. That's true at the companies as well. I once asked Mike Brown, the CFO at Microsoft, who he thought was doing the best work on the stock, and he told me Mike Kwatinetz.

In addition to being a superb quantitative analyst, Mike has always been able to add the qualitative side. Good investments rest not only in being able to read a financial statement but in being able to read people and organizations. When you're investing, the people are paramount. When you invest in a Microsoft or a Dell, you're investing your money *with* Bill Gates or *with* Michael Dell, and with their respective management teams. There are so many intangibles in running each of these businesses that you have to make something of a leap of faith. You have to believe that the guys running the business will, when push comes to shove, make the right decisions. You have to feel confident that they are the type of people you feel comfortable investing your money with for the long run. Finding market-leading companies, with a properly leveraged business model, run by extraordinary people is a tough combination to beat.

I remember that a number of years ago, there was a really hot networking company I kept getting calls about. Everyone was telling me, "If you own Cisco, you have to own this." I went out to see this company. I knew within the first 20 minutes that not only was I never going to own this stock, it was probably one of the great *shorts* of all time—which subsequently proved to be correct.

The stock market today is more volatile than ever, and it's easy to get preoccupied with short-term performance and lose sight of your true objectives. *The Big Tech Score* provides readers with a rare opportunity—the opportunity to gain insight into an investment process that works, from one of Wall Street's true superstars.

The Big Tech Score is an easily read, common-sense approach to technology investing. Mike and I have very consistent views as to how individuals should assess, monitor, and maintain their own investments. They're all laid out in this book—buy what you know, honestly analyze your own risk profile, look for an extraordinary management team, analyze a company's true competitive advantage, look for companies that customers love, monitor their progress, and *stay the course.*

Staying the course is critical. I believe more people make more money on their homes than they do trading or playing the stock market. Why? Because people own their homes for an average of seven years, but they own their stocks for about seven *weeks.* The big returns don't happen in the third week or the third month; the third or fourth year is when you really begin to reap the benefits of a well-placed investment. I read recently that the average turnover for stocks on the Nasdaq is something like *39 days.* I think that if people would commit to a more realistic time horizon when they invest in companies, they'd be much better off.

The Big Tech Score is one of those five or six must reads that should be in everyone's personal investment library. It provides a framework for how to think about investing. It rescues investors from having to be so preoccupied with the day-to-day-ness of the marketplace and teaches them how to think analytically about companies and their true long-term prospects.

Scott W. Schoelzel
Portfolio Manager, Janus Twenty Fund

Preface

I n the winter of 1990, fresh from the sale of the computer consulting firm I'd run for 10 years and itching for a new challenge, I set out to conquer Wall Street. I came armed with a PhD in mathematical modeling, an MBA in accounting, and whatever knowledge I'd gleaned from 15 years of designing software and computer application systems.

I had lots of gumption but absolutely no Wall Street experience. Sanford Bernstein, a respected investment boutique specializing in detailed industry research and evaluation, was looking for a stock research analyst to specialize in the computer industry. I somehow charmed my way into an interview and was hired.

After nine months of work on my first report, I launched as an analyst on January 2, 1991, with a 234-page market research forecast on the PC software industry. I was under the microscope from the start. My analysis of Microsoft especially generated a lot of heat. Word on the Street was that Microsoft's 1992 fiscal earnings would be about $3.70 per share (this was the average or *consensus* estimate amongst sell-side analysts, a number like those often printed in the *Wall Street Journal, New York Times,* and other publications). My report placed them at $4.76, a significant difference considering that most estimates varied by no more than $0.10 or $0.20 from the consensus.

Because I worked for Sanford Bernstein, my analysis couldn't be completely dismissed. But my findings were met with considerable skepticism. How could a new analyst be right when he disagreed so dramatically with all his more senior colleagues? How could a billion-dollar company like Microsoft continue to grow at such a fast rate? Most analysts thought it inevitable that Microsoft stock would begin to slow down. My prediction meant an increase in earnings per share of more than 40 percent over the next year. The pressure was on.

Soon, even I started to doubt my analysis. Sure, I'd been careful, but maybe I'd missed something. Things hit rock bottom when I learned that an important client had asked one of the Bernstein salespeople, "What was Mike smoking when he came up with these numbers?"

I decided to face things head-on. I asked the salesperson to set up a meeting with that client, a brilliant investor named Glenn Doshay who was then at Ardsley Partners and now runs his own firm, Palantir Capital.

Glenn agreed to meet me because, if I was right, Microsoft stock was worth quite a bit more than the price at which it was trading; his company could reap huge profits. The salesman warned that Glenn would grill me mercilessly. I clung to the hope that I held a considerable ace in the hole: I actually thought the *right* Microsoft estimate was $5.40. Worried that something might go wrong, I'd made my model more conservative. Barring an unforeseen disaster, if my work was correct, Microsoft would exceed my estimate considerably.

As a new analyst, I also had somewhat of an edge. I'd had the luxury of spending nine months working exclusively on my research. Once analysts officially launch, they spend a good chunk of their time meeting with institutional accounts, pitching potential investment banking clients, and "firefighting"—responding to the various issues and miniemergencies that arise each day. Only a fraction of their day is available for research. When an analyst is producing his or her initial work, however, none of these distractions exist.

As the new kid on the block, I had triple the number of hours that my competitors had to spend picking apart Microsoft. On the other hand, as veterans they had had years of experience reading the nuances of company signals, learning what might go wrong, seeing how model projections could be missed, and so on. As my meeting with Glenn approached, I double-checked my work, fearing that I might have overlooked an obvious risk that would make me look ridiculous and sabotage my fledgling career.

Glenn's firm, Ardsley, was a hedge fund which traded large amounts of stock continuously and often shorted stocks (selling shares that it didn't own—betting that the price would go down and that it could then *cover* or buy the shares back at this lower value) in order to hedge its bets. Because they trade so frequently, hedge funds tend to aggressively seek every bit of incremental information. Funds that hold stocks for longer periods often act more conservatively and may not be as concerned with acting on a hot but unproven analyst tip.

Before the meeting, I tried to think of every tough question that could possibly be asked. The meeting began and I sat in front of Glenn's desk while he remained behind it. All through our conversation, Glenn continued to check the Reuters quotes and news releases being spit out of his PC, and frequently picked up the phone to give buy or sell orders. For my part, I led him step by step through the assumptions and analyses incorporated into my models. Each time I'd start to think he wasn't paying attention to me, he'd let loose with a series of sharp questions that showed he hadn't missed a thing. After about an hour, Glenn turned to the salesperson and said, "He could be right."

His vote of semiconfidence qualified me for my next inquisitor: Roger McNamee, who at the time was running the Science & Technology Fund for T. Rowe Price. (Roger and John Powell have since started their own firm, Integral Capital Partners, which invests in technology stocks and engages in mezzanine financing, putting money into private companies that are getting close to the initial public offering stage. Roger is perhaps the most widely quoted person on Wall Street, even though his "Wall Street" firm is located 3,000 miles away, in the heart of California's Silicon Valley.)

When a new analyst meets with a Roger McNamee or a Glenn Doshay (or any number of other savvy investors), they have to earn their spurs. Having succeeded with Glenn, I felt pretty good. After meeting with Roger, I was wrung out. It became obvious that no matter how much I'd prepared, there were things I didn't know.

Investors in Roger's funds are a virtual *Who's Who* of technology executives. As a result, he has a timely and formidable base of broad and detailed knowledge. He caught me with my pants down at least once, with questions I hadn't even considered. I did my best to keep up. At the end of the hour-and-a-half meeting, to my relief, Roger told his salesperson that I knew what I was talking about.

Getting the endorsement of Glenn Doshay and Roger McNamee was like a rite of passage. I was off and running in the PC software category—and when Microsoft results for fiscal 1992 met my secret estimate of $5.40, I was officially anointed and on my way.

A WORD ON OUR ADVICE

The technology sector is an extremely fast-paced business. The stock prices for the companies I describe in this book were constantly changing during the course of its writing and production. Because of that, on one page, I may say, for example, that Microsoft is trading at $110 per share, while on another page I place the stock as trading at $80. Huge developments take place in technology on a daily basis, and such changes are nearly inevitable. Between the dates of finishing the manuscript and going to press, major events occurred (for example, PaineWebber, as I predicted, was acquired, and Microsoft lost its first round with the Department of Justice). It's next to impossible to provide up-to-the-minute numbers in a printed format, but the advice contained within these pages should stand you in good stead, regardless of what the market is doing at any given time.

Acknowledgments

A lot went on behind the scenes to make this book a reality. First of all, Danielle and I would like to thank Joy Tutela and everyone else at the David Black literary agency, for believing in this book in its infancy and delivering it into the right hands. We just hope that Joy hasn't learned so much about investing that she decides to leave her day job (and us agentless). Thanks also to Debra Englander, our editor, for her excitement about our ideas, and much help in fleshing them out.

I've been lucky enough to work with some of the smartest people in the business and even luckier that many of them agreed to be quoted in this book. First and foremost, thanks to Scott Schoelzel—you continuously amaze me with your insight into the people and stories behind the stocks. I've also kept counsel with some of the best and brightest Wall Street has to offer. Six (in addition to Scott) contributed greatly to this book: Tom Kamp, Mark Kingdon, Fred Kobrick, Roger McNamee, Quint Slattery (one of my partners), and Larry Solomon.

I would never have gotten to the place I am today without the good fortune to have worked with the people behind some of the most incredible tech companies ever. Hopefully, after reading this, they'll all still be talking to me. Thanks especially to the past and present executives at Allaire, Apple, BSQUARE, Compaq, Dell,

Gateway, Handspring, Hewlett-Packard, IBM, Liberate, Microsoft, Network Associates, Onyx, VA Linux, and Wind River.

Thanks to Christine Ivanov, who holds my life together and who's created every great graphic I've ever used. Thanks to Hans Roderich, who's been my partner in crime for much of the research contained in this book. And thanks to my other partners at Azure—Paul Ferris, Cameron Lester, and Paul Weinstein—I'm looking forward to incredible things.

Thanks to Mike Greenstein, who, despite his skepticism, introduced us to our agent. Thanks to Lee Spelman and Joel Pitt for reading the book and helping correct just a few of our mistakes. And thanks especially to Don Katz, for fantastic advice and invaluable support.

Most of all, thank you to Eric—not only for his insights, but for agreeing to many months of no social life. And thanks to Michelle, my wife and partner, for contributing to making this book happen in more ways than can be mentioned.

The Big
Tech Score

CHAPTER ONE

THE BIG TECH SCORE THEORY OF INVESTING

As a Wall Street analyst, I've had the good fortune to be one of a few select people granted consistent access to the strategic thinking at a number of high-flying technology companies. Every week, I spend close to 70 hours living, breathing, studying, and talking about these companies with the smartest investors in the world. Over time, I've come to believe that there are certain attributes that the best companies share. It doesn't hurt to have spent every day for nearly 10 years observing two of the most successful companies of our era, Microsoft and Dell Computer Corporation.

Many people can't resist the thought of big money, and there's no denying that playing the stock market can sometimes lead to juicy rewards. But stocks are serious business and dabblers often get burned. Winning in the stock market requires discipline, hard work, and focus.

Identifying great companies is only the first step. An even greater challenge is deciding whether to stick with them when you're already ahead 200, 300, or even 500 percent. Take Dell, for example. Someone who invested $10,000 in Dell in 1994 and cashed out when they had a five-bagger (five times the investment, or $50,000) would have missed the opportunity to watch that initial $10,000 shoot up to $1 million in less than five years.

The amateurs aren't the only ones who missed that boat. Believe it or not, many analysts and portfolio managers found it just as difficult to stay with Dell over the long haul. I've had the good sense to stick fast to Dell and Microsoft as they became 10-baggers, 20-baggers, and, in Dell's case, over a 100-bagger. These stocks hit some low points, believe me. But if you know what to look for in a company, even as the media trumpets its downfall and everyone else is scrambling to sell, then it shouldn't matter what conventional wisdom says about it—you've got the tools required to judge for yourself. This book will provide you with those tools so that you will never be dependent on "expert" advice again. You'll *be* the expert.

THE GAME PLAN

1. Read the book.
2. Do the homework.
3. Pick 4 to 7 stocks for your portfolio.
4. Commit to 10 hours a month following them.

A FEW KEY POINTS

Sound investing can make you more money than you could ever hope to save from your job. And a few percentage points difference in annual return can mean big bucks over time. A 30-year-old woman who invests $10,000 and earns a 6 percent return (about average for low-risk bonds) until she is 65 will have a yield of $77,000. A 12 percent compound annual return (the average return for stocks over the past 50 years) on the same initial investment will give that same woman a nest egg worth $528,000 come retirement.

Pretty good, but still not up to our standards. I want your stock investments to yield a *25 percent* return, and this book is going to help you achieve those results. It takes a little bit more work, but I think it's worth it. How worth it? Had that same woman invested the

FIGURE **1.1**   RETIREMENT NEST EGG RESULTS.

AGE	INVESTMENT	RETURN	RESULT AT 65
30	$10,000	6%	$ 77,000
30	10,000	12	528,000
30	10,000	25	24,000,000

initial $10,000 the *big tech score* way, her money would have ballooned to more than $24 million come retirement time (see Figure 1.1).

NO PAIN, NO GAIN?

Winning in the stock market is kind of like losing weight. A consistent, steady approach can yield great results, but everyone will try to convince you that it's all or nothing—"No pain, no gain" and all that. Just as an inactive 500-pound person should not begin a diet regime by trying to run a 26-mile race, an amateur investor shouldn't begin his or her stock experience by throwing money into 20 or 30 stocks.

To win on Wall Street you don't need to start with a huge bankroll. You don't need to listen 24-7 to *Moneyline* or memorize the *Wall Street Journal.* You don't need to be up on every industry coming down the pipe or informed about every merger and acquisition taking place. What you need to do is focus. Take the phrase "jack-of-all-trades, master of none" to heart. It's better to know a lot about a little than a little about a lot. Choose a handful of stocks, dedicate at least 10 hours a month to following them, and make yourself an expert.

THE SEVEN SECRET

How many is too many? I'm a professional analyst. I spend nearly 70 hours each week analyzing stocks. I have people working for me to help weed through the plethora of information. I have access to top management and resources that will be a challenge for you to acquire. Still, even with all of these advantages, I feel that the maximum number of stocks I can thoroughly follow is 15. And that's the maximum—I try to keep it between 10 and 12.

Presumably you have a job and a string of other commitments. You're functioning at less than half my capacity. The number of stocks you own should be a reflection of the amount of time you can dedicate to following them. When you're creating your stock portfolio you should be thinking in the 4- to 7-stock range. That's the maximum number of companies that you have a *chance* of following well.

If you have less than 10 hours a month to devote to research, buy fewer stocks. This will increase your risk. But I'd prefer that you own two stocks and know them inside out to your owning seven and not really understanding any of them.

WHY YOU CAN BEAT THE PROS

I'm a big fan of diversity. I've been able to be pretty aggressive with my stock portfolio because it's only a small portion of my savings. The rest of my money is in "safer" things, such as mutual funds or bonds (covered in more detail in Chapter 2). That said, the stock portion of my investment pool has left the other portions in the dust. Part of this is due to unheard of stock performance during the 1990s, but a lot of it has to do with focus. My mutual fund manager and I may be playing the same market, but we're playing an entirely different game. So are you.

DAVID AND GOLIATH

When it comes to investing, the professionals have the home-field advantage. Mutual fund managers get information faster than you do; they spend all of their time submerged in the stock market; they have professional analysts advising them; and they pay virtually no commission when they trade stocks.

Given all of these advantages, how can you hope to outperform the professionals? Your amateur status entitles you to benefits the pros can't enjoy. Let me explain.

Oddly enough, your edge primarily stems from Securities and Exchange Commission (SEC) regulations designed to protect individual investors. These regulations force portfolio managers to diversify in order to limit the risk to their customers that could be caused by one or two major investment mistakes. Fund managers are forced to spread risk, and they typically do that by buying 100 or more stocks—the larger the fund, the larger the number of stocks it holds.

You can beat the pros for two major reasons. First, you can keep your portfolio limited to a handful of stocks—the best of the best. SEC regulations may limit portfolio managers, but they don't touch you in the least. Second, you're not under pressure to show performance every quarter. That's a huge advantage.

Let's say, for argument's sake, that it was clear in advance what next year's 20 best-performing stocks would be. Because of the limitations we've discussed, portfolio managers have to pick 100 or more stocks, so they have to choose at least 80 beyond those 20 best. You, on the other hand, can limit yourself to 6 or 7 of the top-20 elite. As a result, even if every stock's performance doesn't live up to predictions, you're likely to outdo the portfolio manager if you manage to pick just one or two superior performers. Here's an example:

Let's say that last year you really believed in the power of the Internet. You chose six stocks. Two of them were Cisco and Amazon.

With only six stocks in total, Cisco and Amazon make up one-third of your portfolio. For top mutual funds, the likelihood of the two together comprising even 5 percent of the portfolio are very small. If they did, they would probably have to occupy the two highest positions in the fund.

Because I revel in the unlikely, let's say Cisco and Amazon *do* occupy those top two positions, and assume that over the year the two stocks double. This gives the fund 5 percent performance on the whole. If the rest of the portfolio goes up 10 percent, the total return would be 14½ percent for the year (see Figure 1.2). So Cisco and Amazon are responsible for pushing the fund's performance up from 10 to 14½ percent.

Now compare these figures to your own portfolio. Let's say that you invested $60,000 in your six stocks. If you had invested an

FIGURE 1.2   DAVID AND GOLIATH FUND PERFORMANCE.

PARAMETER	CISCO AND AMAZON	REST OF PORTFOLIO	TOTAL PORTFOLIO
$100 Million Fund			
Investment, $	5 million	95 million	100 million
Return, %	100%	10%	14.5%
Return, $	5.0 million	9.5 million	14.5 million
$60,000 Individual Portfolio			
Investment, $	20,000	40,000	60,000
Return, %	100%	10%	40%
Return, $	20,000	4,000	24,000

equal amount of money in all six stocks, and Cisco and Amazon were two of them, then if they doubled you would make $20,000 on the $20,000 you invested in the two. Your other four stocks combined would account for $40,000 of your initial investment. If you picked mediocre performers that average a 10 percent return, you would make only an additional $4,000 from those four stocks.

Here's where being David works in your favor. Consider: Even with the ho-hum foursome, you've made *40 percent* on your portfolio. The spectacular performance of Cisco and Amazon added only 4½ percent to the mutual fund's portfolio, but it added 30 percent to yours. Because your stock investments are so selective, you get a lot more leverage out of those two stocks than Goliath does.

Over the past four years, my highest-rated stocks have appreciated at an average compound rate of over 100 percent per year. I'm going to offer you a unique set of rules that have been the backbone of my good fortune. The good news is that you can learn the rules rather easily. The bad news is that you have to do your own homework. I'll show you the method, but you'll have to work hard to apply it.

As mentioned, I want you to spend at least 10 hours a month keeping up with your stocks. If you do, you'll actually be spending *more* time per stock than most portfolio managers. Your 10 hours a month will give you almost 2 hours to focus on each of the stocks in your portfolio. A portfolio manager would be lucky to get in an hour of work on each. If a manager owns 120 stocks and works a 60-hour week, that's about all he or she can hope for, because managers are unlikely to spend even half their time tracking stocks they own.

BOOT CAMP

Lots of investors treat the market like a trip to the horse races. They want someone to give them a tip that's a "sure thing" so that they can put down some cash. Unfortunately, there are no sure things, and most tips will fail. Winning in the stock market takes research and diligence. If you're not prepared to invest your time before you invest your money, don't bother with this book. Don't make anyone—your broker, your friends, or me—responsible for your investments.

On the other hand, if you *are* ready, this book will help you. Think of it as boot camp. Leave your ego at the door, take a deep breath, and get ready to work. Make no mistake, you *will* work. Your broker, your financial magazine, your Uncle Morty—whoever it is you traditionally turn to for investment advice—has been functioning as your investment security blanket. You're probably used to getting advice and deciding whether to act upon it, but you're not used to doing the work yourself. Well it's time for a little spring cleaning. I want you to ditch the security blanket and learn to generate your *own* advice. That's what boot camp's about.

I guarantee there will be moments when you want to throw this book across the room and go AWOL. One more rule, one more formula, one more tip thrown your way—let's face it, boot camp is a bitch. But stick it out. I promise you'll leave stronger, leaner, tougher, and prepared for anything the market can throw your way.

WHY THIS BOOK?

Three years ago, my daughter came to me for advice. She had some money and wanted to know how to invest it. I'm your typical protective father, so I wanted to pick some certain winners. Of course there's no such thing as a sure bet in the stock market, but I tried to funnel my knowledge to come as close as possible.

The results weren't too shabby—her money increased sixfold in only three years' time. But the problem was, she wasn't satisfied. She wanted to learn to do things herself.

We began talking about what it is that makes a stock great. And Danielle started taking notes. Eventually, we got to thinking that the tips I was laying at her feet might be worth sharing with others. A book was born.

Let me state for the record that the thing that makes me so good at my job is that I'm extremely left-brained. While my own writing may rivet the attention of professionals, it elicits yawns from general readers. So my daughter and I made a deal: I'd dole out the advice and she'd make it potable. Throughout this book we'll be writing from my point of view even though the pen is hers.

WHY MATH IS GOOD FOR YOU

So many people are afraid of numbers. In a world of instant gratification, it's hard to find people willing to roll up their sleeves, sharpen their pencils, and bear down. Like it or not, to ditch the security blanket completely, you have to do some math. But rest assured, while there's a lot of math in this book, none of it extends past eighth-grade arithmetic. I've done regression analysis, multivariant analysis, and a slew of other heady mathematics. I love to pick apart the present value of discounted cash flow and ruminate about earnings before interest, taxes, depreciation, and amortization (EBITDA), but you don't have to. Danielle made me promise not to alienate readers with my enthusiasm for algorithms, so while there's some multiplication, division, addition, and subtraction, that's about it. For anything harder we provide a worksheet that lets you plug in the numbers.

I've formulated a set of strategies to help you invest wisely. Some are basic philosophy (Chapters 1 to 4) or qualitative rules (Chapters 5 to 8), while others are almost purely number related (Chapters 9 to 11). If the math proves too traumatic, you can skip the quantitative analysis completely and focus on more qualitative measuring sticks. Your stock picks won't be as informed, but they'll still benefit from being screened by a fairly tough set of criteria.

WHAT TO EXPECT

This book has two major purposes: to offer investors advice on overall investment strategy and to offer methods of judging which companies are solid long-term investments. The best way to teach is by example. To that end, the book presents dozens of case studies and explains which companies got things right and which ones blew their opportunities.

I especially focus on Microsoft and Dell and outline why they are poster children for the big tech score theory. I measure them against the methodologies used, both today and several years ago and show you what made me believe in them in the early years and what's kept me on board ever since. Then I talk about the stocks in my own portfolio, as well as Danielle's, and explain how we chose what we did and why (Chapter 12). Finally, I discuss what's coming down the pipe in the next few years: trends you should anticipate and how you should think of them, in light of the overall discussion (Chapters 13 and 14). Hopefully, this will help you find tomorrow's stock superstars.

IN THE MONEY

Lots of kids spend a few years holed away, boning up for their SATs. The math involved in that barbaric bubble test is comparable in difficulty to what is within these pages. But were you to send your kids to their rooms to bone up on the math in this book rather than the math in their SAT prep homework, they'd become rich faster than they ever could by getting a college education.

If your son or daughter mastered the math in this book, and at age 18 you armed him or her with the $100,000 you would have spent on a college education, your kid would be a millionaire before the age of 30—*after* taxes (see Figure 1.3). By 40, he or she would have raked in more than $9 million.

Even a mutual fund would stand the kid in good stead. That $100,000 invested in a good fund when little Johnny reaches his eighteenth birthday will have doubled twice to yield more than four times the money by the time his thirtieth birthday rolls around. When he reaches 40, he'll have $1,545,000 to blow during his midlife crisis.

I tell you this not because I actually expect you to send your teenage daughter to her room clutching this book, but because I want you to understand its power. If your kids can learn the math for the SAT, then you can learn the math within these pages. And believe me, the concepts in this book will improve your financial situation much more than a college diploma ever could.

PLAYING THE STOCK MARKET

If there's one phrase that really annoys me, it's "playing the stock market." Investing in the stock market is not a game, but many people approach it with the same seriousness as they would a Hula-Hoop. Here's some advice: If you want to play with some money,

FIGURE 1.3   AFTER-TAX YIELD ON $100,000 INVESTED AT AGE 18.

	AGE			
RETURN	**30**	**40**	**50**	**60**
15% (good mutual fund)	$ 405,000	$1,545,000	$ 6,160,000	$ 24,827,000
25% (our goal)	1,049,000	9,517,000	88,382,000	822,876,000

take up blackjack. This book is not for you. These methods are for the serious-minded, ready to put their minds and their money to work.

Amateurs make small amounts of money in the stock market all the time. You don't need me for that. My aim is to teach you how to reel in the big fish. I want you to take a chunk of money and target earnings of 25 percent or more per year. Will you earn it on every stock you invest in? If you did it would be a miracle. Certainly I haven't done so, and neither has anyone I know in the industry. But can you *average* 25 percent on this money? You have a very good shot at it if you follow the advice in this book.

SUMMING UP

- Winning in the stock market requires discipline, hard work, and focus.
- Dedicate at least 10 hours a month to keeping up with your portfolio.
- Limit your holdings to a maximum of seven stocks.
- Aim for a return of 25 percent or more on your stock investments.
- Remember: You need only two superstars to win big.

CHAPTER TWO

CONCENTRATE YOUR INVESTMENTS ON A HANDFUL OF COMPANIES

A 50-year-old man comes to me for advice. He tells me he's earning $100,000 a year. He's got a pension plan and $200,000 set aside for his golden years. When those years dawn, at 65, he's determined that he'll need $50,000 a year in income in order to meet his needs. He asks me what stocks he should buy.

"None," I answer. He's confused. "Listen," I say. "You're done. You've got the money you need to meet your goal. If you make the mistake of putting your savings into risky ventures when there's no need to do so, you're foolish. Why put your future at risk and take the chance that you'll end up with less than you need?" (See Figure 2.1.)

It amazes me how many people make this mistake. In law there's a famous phrase, "The punishment should fit the crime." I have my own catchphrase for the would-be investor: "The strategy should fit the goal." You wouldn't give a jaywalker a 10-year sentence. It just doesn't make sense. Likewise, a 60-year-old who wants to retire in style shouldn't place his or her entire nest egg in high-risk stocks. It just doesn't make sense. The strategy should fit the goal.

FIGURE 2.1   RETIREMENT PICTURE FOR 50-YEAR-OLD
EARNING $100,000 WITH $200,000
SAVINGS AND A PENSION PLAN.

PARAMETER	PENSION PLAN	CURRENT SAVINGS	ADDITIONAL ANNUAL SAVINGS	TOTAL
Current amount	NA	$200,000	$10,000	
Earnings per year to 65	NA	5% (tax free)	5% (tax free)	
Capital at 65	NA	$400,000	$225,000	$625,000
Earnings on capital		6% (taxable)	6% (taxable)	
Income at 65	$20,000	$24,000	$13,500	$57,500

It's much harder to hit a target when you don't know what you're aiming for. Before investing a dime, it's important that you sit down and decide on your investment goals.

Imagine yourself at retirement. How much money do you need to live the way you'd like? Once you've got a number in your head, ask yourself if you can get there without taking a lot of risk. Can you meet your goals by putting the money you currently have saved into something with a 6 percent return? If so, put the amount you need into something safe before you even *think* of playing the market. You can risk any money *in excess* of that original amount without jeopardizing your retirement.

CREATING INVESTMENT POOLS

Diversity is a big buzzword in the investment world. And why not? Diversifying your investment portfolio gives you a greater measure of safety. The problem is, too many people aim for diversity in the wrong place. They throw money into a truckload of stocks all across the market in order to safeguard themselves. As far as I'm concerned, that's not diversity, that's stupidity.

The most important advice I can possibly give you is this: Forget the bloated stock portfolio; get your diversity by buying bonds and mutual funds. Then take a *portion* of your investment money—a portion you're willing to risk—and focus it on that magic six or seven.

Dividing the money you have available for investment into three pools—stocks, mutual funds, and safe money—gives you the security you need to approach the stock market in the right way. Your allotment for each investment pool will depend on several things: your age, your income, your investment objective, and how much time you have to devote to investment research. Although every person is different, Figure 2.2 will give you a rough idea.

POOL 1: SAFE MONEY

By *safe* money, I mean tax-free bonds, treasuries, and other investments that reliably turn out interest. The numbers vary from time to time, but 6 percent is a typical average annual return. The major benefit of the 6 percent return is security.

FIGURE 2.2   ROUGH IDEA OF INVESTMENT POOL STRATEGY.

	INVESTMENT ALLOCATION, %		
AGE	SAFE MONEY	MUTUAL FUNDS	STOCKS
20	0	70	30
30	10	60	30
40	20	60	20
50	40	40	20
60	60	20	20
65	70	15	15

As you age, you should increase this pool's percentage in your portfolio. This is important, because—like it or not—*you don't have as many years to play the odds.*

Sound investing can create more wealth than you can ever hope to save from your job, but time is of the essence. Sock money away while you're young, and a few percentage points difference in annual return can mean big bucks come retirement.

A 30-year-old who invests $10,000 and earns a 6 percent return will have a yield of $77,000 by retirement. At a 12 percent return per year, the same $10,000 investment would swell to $528,000. These are no small potatoes.

But if you wait too long to start saving for retirement, compounding has less of an effect. It takes awhile for interest to accumulate, and if you start at age 60, rather than at 30, the difference between a 6 percent and a 12 percent return is not as great (see Figure 2.3). Since the market can't be counted on to perform normally in every five-year period, betting on those few percentage points isn't always worth the risk.

Safe money should always be a chunk of your portfolio. But as retirement looms, the chunk should grow. Once you're 55 or older, this pool by itself, with the return expected, should be enough to meet your retirement objectives. It may not be as racy an investment, but it's a smart one—and smart, as they say, is sexy.

Hopefully, the older you are, the closer you are to your retirement objective. Once you're old enough for the senior citizen's discount, you should be in good stead. If you've been saving diligently, a 6 percent return should do for you. But if this is not the

FIGURE 2.3   INVESTMENT RESULTS AT AGE 65.

		YIELD AT AGE 65	
INITIAL AGE	**INITIAL AMOUNT**	**6% RETURN**	**12% RETURN**
30	$10,000	$77,000	$528,000
60	10,000	13,382	17,623

case, if you look at that 6 percent return and can't envision any chance of it producing the results you need, you're going to have to either reset your objectives or take on more risk.

POOL 2: MUTUAL FUNDS

This pool provides what I call *typical* stock market return. Pick a decent fund and your money will earn what the market does— your earnings will rise when the market rises and fall when it falls. All fund managers are not created equal. Because of that, I like to diversify within this field—just in case I happen to pick a clunker. There's safety in numbers.

Even with a handful of mutual funds, performance isn't guaranteed. Over the past 50 years, the stock market as a whole has had an average annual return of 12 percent. Unfortunately, over any given three-, five-, six-, or seven-year period this can vary quite a bit. When you put money into the market, you want it to be money you don't need to touch. Over time, the law of averages tends to work out, but in a short span—and a short span for the market may be half a decade—it might not work out the way you'd like.

To better understand how results can deviate in a short period of time, consider the probability that a tossed coin will come up heads. We all know it's 50 percent. Now flip a coin once. I guarantee that you won't have 50 percent heads. Flip it 100 times and you're likely to get closer.

Investing in the stock market is like betting on a coin toss. Put probability on your side. When you're thinking of putting money into the market, don't think in terms of less than 10 years.

A Note on Mutual Funds

If you're aiming for a 12 or 15 percent return on your money, you don't need me, you need a good mutual fund. *Money* magazine routinely does roundups of the best mutual funds, outlining their benefits and drawbacks. Get a copy and make a few phone calls. Do it yourself; don't use a broker. Brokers have a vested interest in making money. They get paid by generating commissions, so it's not in their best interest to recommend mutual funds that have no fees attached. If you're going to ask a broker for advice, then you should expect to pay for that advice, just as you would pay a lawyer or an accountant.

The best way to earn 12 percent on your money is to put it into an index mutual fund. These funds buy all of the stocks in the Standard & Poor's (S&P) 500 Stock Index, in proportion to their piece of the S&P. These funds therefore appreciate at exactly the same rate as the market. An index fund should charge you virtually no fees, because it doesn't have to pay analysts or portfolio managers. It should be a no-load fund (no up-front charge to you) with extremely low annual fees.

Moving up the ladder, we have the 15 percent return. I'm still talking about mutual funds, but not index funds. To outperform the average market return of 12 percent, you need to find a fund that is managed by a savvy portfolio manager. Over a long period of time, the best portfolio managers can earn 15 percent or more per year.

How do you find the best? Some of the strongest portfolio managers in the business are quoted in this book—you can start by looking at their funds. But don't take my word for it—do your homework. You can request records on one-, three-, and five-year performance directly from any fund. There's also a completely independent company, Morningstar, that tracks the performance of all the major players. Intuit offers the latest Morningstar ratings as part of its Quicken software product. Get the past year's back issues of *Money* from the library, and start studying.

The Dog Ate My Homework

It's so easy and beneficial to do this homework, and yet few people are willing to put in the time. It may seem easier to stick with the 12 percent return instead of bothering with all the research involved to achieve the elusive 15 percent. After all, 3 percent may not seem like a big deal. How much is doing your homework really worth? If I were to tell you that someone was willing to pay you $1,000 an hour for a bit of reading, would you consider that a good rate of pay? Of course you would.

FIGURE 2.4 FUTURE VALUE OF $10,000 AT
VARYING RATES OF RETURN.

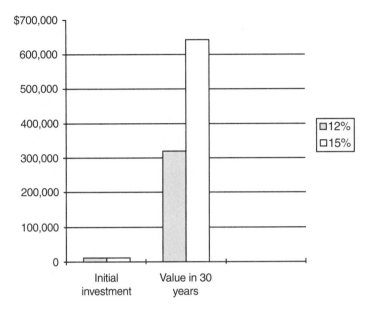

Let's say you were to put in $10,000 up front and earn 15 per-
cent annually on it over a 30-year period. You'd make *$320,000*
more than if you'd earned only 12 percent (see Figure 2.4). If you
spend a mere 20 hours of work looking at Morningstar reports and
Money magazine to find the best funds and then 10 hours a year to
keep tabs on things, you will earn about $1,000 an hour. That's not
too shabby.

POOL 3: STOCKS

The third pool is stocks, the riskiest of the three. But if you've covered yourself in the other two areas, you'll have the safety net you
need to invest here in earnest. This book is focused on optimizing
your returns from this third pool, so I won't get into it here. Let
me just lay out a few overall investment ground rules.

SCARED MONEY RARELY WINS

Too many people invest with what I refer to as *scared money*. They're taking the rent money and investing! A friend of mine came to me and said, "Mike, I want to buy a house in six months. I've got enough money set aside for the down payment. Tell me what stocks I should put it in for the six months so I can have some appreciation." And my answer was "*None.*"

To play the market with a six-month result in mind, you've got to be out of your mind. How can anyone know for certain what's going to happen in those six months? What are you going to do if the stock goes down 25 percent and you don't have enough money left for your down payment? This is not a sensible way to invest.

People who invest in order to meet an imperative at the end of a short-term period often get in over their heads. They buy the stock at a premium, something happens, and the stock price drops. The six months are up, they need the money, and they're forced to sell it when the price is low.

TIMING IS EVERYTHING

The most important element to understand when investing your money is the power of time. If I could teach investors only one thing, it would be to use time to your advantage and never get into a situation where time is against you.

The key rule when making an investment plan is to fill the stock allotment with an amount of money you can handle both going up and going down, because sometimes it *will* go down—a lot. The stocks we're talking about have huge potential for making money for you, but they also have tremendous volatility. At times they can go down 30 to 40 percent over two weeks. But if they're true winners, the reasons won't be based on fundamentals, just a quirk in the market or a trend in the press.

Once you learn to recognize the fundamentals, you can buck the consensus. First you need to know what to look for. Now that we've got the preliminaries out of the way, let's get down to business.

SUMMING UP

- Set an investment objective so that you understand your target.
- Create pools to diversify your investments and limit your risk.
- Don't put scared money into the market.
- Invest your time before you invest your money. Find a good mutual fund and reap the rewards of the extra 3 percent.
- Respect the law of averages—never put money into the stock market if you'll need it in the short term.

CHAPTER THREE

BUY LOW, SELL HIGH

I 'll tell you the key to winning in the stock market if you promise not to laugh: *Buy low, sell high.* True, everyone has heard these magic words, but you'd be hard pressed to find an investor who consistently follows them. The reason? People tend to jump on the bandwagon in either direction. When stocks are low, you don't see the headline "Great Buying Opportunity!" in the *New York Times* or the *Wall Street Journal.* What you read about is why the world is coming to an end, whether because of the Y2K problem, or the Asian crisis, or crumbling financial institutions, or a domino effect out of Russia—*that's* what you read in the press. Your broker calls to tell you to sell. Make no mistake—the reason the market is low is because of all this. It's never low when everybody is superbly optimistic. It's low when pessimism reigns supreme.

When the market has crumbled, when everyone is shouting "Sell!" and stockbrokers everywhere are crying into their coffee— that, my friend, is the time to buy, and buy a lot.

Why? You've put the seven companies in your portfolio through their paces; you've measured them according to the methods laid out in this book and assessed their worth yourself. Take advantage of your homework: During times of panic, you may have a chance to make 50 percent or more on your stocks in a couple of months. If you've identified six or seven winners, then they're a good buy regardless of the news that's making everyone else nervous. In fact, with everyone bailing out, they're probably a bargain. Switch some funds from your safe-money pool (only an amount that you're positive you can replenish from new savings within *one year*) and buy more shares of those stocks in your portfolio that are the most undervalued. I discuss how to measure this later.

Selling high is trickier, because you should rarely sell the types of stocks we're targeting. You should abandon these stocks only when you determine that the fundamentals are no longer what they were.

There is, however, one exception to this rule: Sometimes high-growth stocks become so incredibly valued, so far askew from how they've ever been valued before, and so far askew from the metrics covered in this book, that you might consider *trimming* a little bit.

Just as when news is bad, everybody wants to sell, when news is good, they all want to buy. Get too many people grabbing at a rising star, and the company's stock often shoots up well beyond what it's worth. It's a simple matter of supply and demand.

If you do the calculations laid out in the following chapters for each of the stocks in your portfolio, you'll have a fairly close idea of the level where each one should be trading. If you wake up one morning to find that one of your picks has flown off the charts for a temporary reason, consider whether you think it's worth the hubbub. If not, it may be time to trim.

When I say you should *trim,* I don't mean that you should bail out of a hotshot stock completely—but don't ignore your analysis.

Let's say, for example, that you've done unbelievably well with Dell. You bought it seven years ago for $5,000. The stock is now worth $750,000—150 times what you paid for it. You have never sold a share.

You look, and according to your analysis and the table on high growth stocks in Chapter 9 (Figure 9.5), you see that Dell is trading 30 percent higher than it should be. It wouldn't be a bad thing at this juncture to sell 20 percent of your position. Again, I'm not telling you to get out of the stock completely. Sell a portion of your shares in the heat of the moment, make a few bucks, and get back in when the frenzy has died down and the shares are trading at a more reasonable level.

These blips tend to pass in a matter of weeks, days, even hours. No matter how fundamentally good a company is, if it doesn't have the revenue to support an astronomical share price, that bubble is going to burst.

FEEDING THE FRENZY

Watching a stock in crisis is a bit like watching a football game. Context is everything. People tend to overreact—they get so upset with a crummy quarter that they convince themselves that the entire game is lost.

When your favorite company is knee-deep in misfortune, it's important not to ride the wave of other people's panic. Instead, ask yourself whether this is a temporary problem or a permanent one.

Don't look to the media to help you. After all, bad news is a hot story. A not-quite crisis doesn't make very good news. Take the Asian Crisis—"Asia Is Collapsing" is a headline. "Asia Is Not So Bad" is not a headline. Tragedy is an attention-grabber, and the media like to write about it.

Industry experts shout crisis for a different reason: It's easier to go with the flow than to fight one's way against a strong current. If everybody's saying that things are awful, most analysts will agree—that way they won't be blamed later for painting too rosy a picture. It's better to overstate a problem than to understate it. At no time in recent years has this lemming phenomenon been more apparent than during the Asian Crisis.

In the mid- to late 1990s, the Asian economy was expanding at a dizzying rate. There was an overwhelming mentality among investors that one *had* to invest in Asia. Asia was gold. In the frenzy to get on board before the opportunity was yanked, lots of investors threw money at incredibly speculative enterprises. More cash flooded into the region than could readily be absorbed. At a certain juncture, the currencies of several Asian countries collapsed; as the economies of those countries fell apart, Wall Street panicked. There was talk of a domino effect.

Asian buying patterns only increased the Street's worry. In many countries, buying slowed down almost to a standstill. Just to give you an idea, at the height of the crisis I ran into an acquaintance who sold helicopters in Asia, and I asked him what kind of a percentage drop in sales he was seeing due to the slowdown, "You don't understand," he said. "Sales are zero. It isn't just a percentage. It's zero."

Now, to most consumers, buying computers is more important than buying a helicopter, but even so, tech companies were in trouble. Local people being paid in local currency were suddenly making a third in U.S. dollars of what they had been making just a few months before. If they wanted to buy PCs priced in dollars, the purchase was now three times more expensive than it had been before the crisis hit.

Think about this in terms of a car: If a Japanese car had been selling for $15,000 yesterday, and today the same car was selling for $45,000, you might not buy a car for awhile. The same thing happened in many countries in Asia. PC companies that had been making a good chunk of their revenue by exporting to Asia found that many of those markets just ceased to exist.

Wall Street did not take the news well. Everybody panicked, and tech stocks took a dive. Certain analysts began predicting that the PC market was going to die because of what was happening in Asia and the Pacific region. By the end of 1997, tech stocks had hit rock bottom.

I found myself virtually alone in feeling incredulous. It seemed absolutely loony to me that analysts would be loudly proclaiming doomsday without first analyzing the depth of the problem. As I saw incredible tech stocks trading in the basement, all I could think to say to my clients was "Buy—buy a lot."

At the heart of my calm was a feeling that everyone was overreacting. When you're valuing a stock, you should be looking at more than the next three months, more than the next quarter, or even more than the next year—you should be looking at the *entire future* of that company. You should be looking at not just one opportunity, but at multiple opportunities. With this in mind, I urged my clients to think about two things:

- Is the problem in Asia a temporary phenomenon or a permanent one?
- Is the problem as big as Wall Street thinks?

A look at PC sales worldwide showed anyone calm enough to notice that Asia was only one of many high-yield opportunities for technology companies. Worry had caused a depreciation in tech stocks that was totally out of proportion to the magnitude of the problem. True, Asia made up roughly 23 percent of PC sales worldwide. But Europe, which traditionally made up an almost identical percentage of sales, was just then emerging from a slump. Improved sales on the Continent had the potential to offset the decline in Asia.

And what about Asia? While it was true that the Pacific region as a whole was experiencing a decline in sales, it didn't look so bad country by country. Japan made up about 10 percent of Asian PC demand, and while sales there were flat, they were stable. Demand in China, with the second-largest market in Asia, was actually *growing*. Sales in India and Australia were on the rise as well.

Looking at the situation country by country, it was clear that the "crisis" was overstated. Wall Street was focusing its attention on Taiwan, Korea, and Malaysia, but even if sales in those countries dropped to next to null, overall worldwide demand wouldn't be affected by more than 1 to 2 percent. Europe and the rest of Asia would make up for the shortfall. My view was that the upcoming year (1998) would be an average year for PC sales, not a tragic one. And if I was right, tech stocks were actually a bargain, with the prices being so low because everyone was anticipating a collapse. It was time to buy like crazy.

GETTING SPECIFIC

Bad news doesn't always plague an entire industry. More often, it is company specific. But a little floundering can work in your favor. Getting into a long-term stock during a downturn can significantly improve your profits. Following are a few examples of bad news that made for great buying opportunities.

MICROSOFT

In December 1997, the Department of Justice (DOJ) obtained a temporary injunction to prevent Microsoft from shipping its Windows operating system bundled with its Internet Explorer browser. The DOJ felt that this exclusive arrangement was monopolistic. On the heels of the announcement, Microsoft stock took a huge hit. Many investors felt that Microsoft was going down. In reality, the injunction was no big deal.

Microsoft was a powerhouse—it had the money and the wherewithal to fight the system. Plus, anyone following Microsoft knew that a new version of Windows (Windows 98) would be released in a few months. Investors who bothered to look at the company's history would have seen that every single past product release had affected Microsoft stock favorably. Armed with that knowledge, smart investors worked the DOJ announcement; while everyone else was panicking, they bought Microsoft cheap, knowing that the stock would probably rise when Windows 98 shipped.

If you had been this smart investor, you would have bought the stock at around 70 and seen it shoot past 100 only four months later. You would not, as most people did, have bought it in June, when Microsoft won an appeal of the temporary injunction and the stock soared (see Figure 3.1).

Repeat after me: *Buy low, sell high.* Do not buy when everyone is euphoric. Buy when everyone is scared.

GATEWAY

Gateway didn't start the new millennium off with a bang, it started it with a whimper. In January, the company publicly announced that it had failed to meet the numbers it had promised investors for the end of fiscal year 1999.

Gateway had a story—there's always a story. No company wants you to believe that its revenue growth is rapidly decreasing, so companies give things a spin.

Now, I like Gateway. It's not a high-growth company (in this book's definition of the term), but it's a strong one. The company has good products and an excellent management team. All the fundamentals are there.

FIGURE 3.1   THE RISE (AND FALL) OF MICROSOFT.

A few examples of how news has affected Microsoft's share price*:	
June 1998	A federal appeals court lifts a previous injunction that restricted the sale of Windows 95 bundled with Internet Explorer. Shares jump over 20 points, from 84 to 105.
November 1999	Judge Jackson issues his findings of fact, using the term *monopoly power* more than two dozen times in his short statement. Microsoft trading is five times normal volume the day of the announcement, with 122 million shares changing hands.
March 2000	Microsoft moves to settle. On the news, shares rise 10 points to 112 by the end of the month.
April 3, 2000	Shares plummet to 90 on news that Jackson will rule.
April 24, 2000	Shares drop down to 66.50 when the government announces it will push for the breakup of Microsoft.
June 2000	Microsoft declares it will appeal Jackson's decision to break the company in two by taking the case to the Supreme Court. The stock rises to 80 on the news.

*All share prices adjusted for splits

Gateway's spin on the missed quarter was that it wasn't the company's fault. Gateway blamed an Intel chip shortage and the Taiwan earthquake. I wanted to believe that Gateway's low revenue in the previous quarter had been a temporary glitch due to things beyond the company's control. I wanted to believe this because if it were true, it would be a great time for my clients to buy Gateway stock, which had plunged after the announcement.

Gateway's problems had started in early December. Intel ran out of the chips Gateway needed for its high-end machines. Intel assured Gateway that the problem would be solved in time for the Christmas season, but it was tight.

At about the same time, Gateway was dealt another blow. Because of an earthquake in Taiwan, companies were short on components. Prices of DRAM (dynamic random-access memory), a particularly expensive component, shot up drastically.

For those who don't know, Gateway, like Dell, sells computers directly to the public and takes advantage of small inventory. (As discussed in Chapter 6, keeping a smaller inventory is a huge advantage to direct merchants—known as "directs" in the business—because traditionally, the price of components keeps going down). Gateway, as a rule, doesn't hold much DRAM inventory. This usually works in its favor; buying DRAM units later means buying them cheaper. But once in a blue moon a component will spike up in price, and this, according to Gateway, was one of those times.

Christmas shopping season hit, and Gateway still didn't have the chips. The company had placed a sea of ads promising hot new computers built around that specific chip, and while in most seasons customers would be willing to wait until the chips arrived, at Christmas time they were impatient. Gateway lost those sales completely.

There was also another set of customers, customers whose orders had already been processed and who had been promised that machines with the new chip would arrive by Christmas. Gateway, known for its fantastic customer service, couldn't let those customers down, especially during the holidays. So it gave them machines with an even better chip, for the same price. This may have kept customers happy, but it brought Gateway's profits for the quarter down even further.

That was the Gateway story. Did I believe it? Yes. I'd read about the Taiwan earthquake, I'd heard from Dell and other direct sellers that Intel had been short on chips, and I'd looked up DRAM prices on the Internet to see if they had indeed gone up. All of it checked out.

After investigating, I trusted Gateway. I believed that the company's misfortune was a temporary phenomenon, not a permanent one, although the stock did not reflect that. But while I believed Gateway, I felt that some of its problems would persist through the

March quarter. I told my clients to wait until May, by which time I expected that the stock would be at a very attractive price.

HEWLETT-PACKARD

Hewlett-Packard (HP) isn't a high-growth company, but it's a great example of how a stock can take a roller-coaster ride up and down the Dow in a relatively short period of time. To me, HP is the poster child for the importance of buying a stock at the right time.

HP is no VA Linux—it will probably never go up by several hundred percent in a week's time. HP is probably a 10 to 15 percent grower when things are going well, 5 to 10 percent when they're not. The company may not be a hot young thing, but it's been pretty consistent over the past decade or so.

When the Asian Crisis hit, HP was dramatically affected. HP's revenue growth rate went from 10, to 5, to 4 percent, and then sunk close to 1 percent by the end of 1998. Wall Street was looking at those quarters and saying "Things are terrible at HP," and the stock reflected that assessment. It basically collapsed.

Looking at HP in February 1999, I saw things differently. HP was trading at a profit-to-earnings (P/E) ratio of 21, 5 points lower than the average company in the S&P 500.

THE PRICE-TO-EARNINGS (P/E) RATIO

$$\frac{P}{E} = \frac{\text{price of stock}}{\text{one year's earnings per share}}$$

Now HP had had trouble in Asia, no doubt about it, but it was at its heart a strong company, at least as strong as the average S&P corporation. I felt the stock was unfairly underappreciated. If its P/E went up just enough to match the S&P average—in other words, if HP got just a normal P/E ratio, nothing drastic—the stock would go up by 25 percent. And if HP actually showed some growth in the quarter, I thought that many investors and analysts would happily get on board. I told clients to get into HP in February, while it was low.

Five months later, HP's stock had appreciated from $70.50 a share to $107 a share. Why? Well, it wasn't the earnings. The estimated earnings for fiscal 1999 had increased from $3.35 a share to $3.55—only 20 cents—but the P/E had shot up considerably. Now it was 30.1, several points *higher* than the S&P average. The stock's meteoric rise had almost nothing to do with performance and everything to do with perception. Most of the appreciation of the stock happened because the Street was excited about HP again. In my opinion, it was time to sell.

I suggested selling because HP was, at its core, the same company it had been six months before. It was a company growing at 5 to 15 percent annually, and now it was trading at a *premium* to the S&P 500, not a discount. It was no longer a value play.

By November, HP was cheap again. It was a buyer's market. By February 2000 it was time to sell.

IN AND OUT?

Let me be clear: This buy, sell, buy, sell craziness is not what I want you to do with your investments. With high-growth companies, my advice is to buy and hold. However, if you were playing this end of the spectrum, it would be a different story. Holding on tight to stock in a company that's growing only 10 percent a year, the most you can reasonably expect to average over the course of the year is about 10 percent.

Buying low and selling high is the only way to make more on that type of company. It takes a lot of attention—you have to follow the ins and outs like a hawk—but it can make a huge difference in your profits with a slower-growth company.

THE LONG-TERM PORTFOLIO

What I'm trying to teach you is how to be *perverse*. When the news is bad and stocks have reacted accordingly—especially when they have overreacted—it's a great time to buy. Look at your tables and the seven stocks in your portfolio. These should be stocks you know and love. If one of them is trading way below what you've analyzed it to be worth, take advantage of bad news and buy more shares. Invest in the underdog. Don't wait for someone else to anoint your favorite. This book gives you all the tools you need to analyze a stock's worth yourself.

On the other hand, when the news is good and people are euphoric, you may consider trimming your holdings slightly. And please, don't buy—no matter how good the news is. Take these words to heart:

1. Think perversely.
2. Revel in bad news.
3. Get in while the going's bad.

SUMMING UP

- Stocks are never cheap when everyone loves them. They're cheap when pessimism reigns supreme.
- If you've identified six or seven winners, they're a good buy regardless of the news that's making everyone else nervous.
- If everyone is bailing out of a stock in your portfolio (which you've put through the paces laid out in this book) consider taking some funds from your safe-money pool and using them to pay for more shares. Buy low.
- Take out only an amount of safe money that you're positive you can replenish from new savings within *one year.*
- If one of your stocks becomes an overnight sensation, and you determine that it's overvalued, consider trimming your holding. Sell high. Take some profits.
- When you're valuing a stock that's currently in trouble, you should be looking at the entire future of that company, not just the near term. Ask yourself:

  Are its current problems temporary, or permanent?

  Are its problems as big as Wall Street thinks?

Chapter Four

Don't Invest Blindly

Alittle knowledge is a dangerous thing. So is no knowledge. You'd never expect to perform open-heart surgery without going through medical school. You'd never expect to have a conversation in Arabic without learning the language. You'd never expect to argue and win a case before the Supreme Court without poring over a stack of law books. Yet, many investors expect to make a mint by investing in companies completely blindly, with absolutely no knowledge to guide them.

Why do they do it? Oh, many reasons. Sometimes it's overconfidence, sometimes a lack of confidence. Whatever the source, it usually falls under one of the human weaknesses described in this chapter—what I call investment's Seven Deadly Sins.

THE SEVEN DEADLY SINS

1. Hastiness
2. Omission
3. Arrogance
4. Negligence
5. Submissiveness

6. Lethargy

7. Greed

HASTINESS

We're living in an "I've got to have it now!" era—and never before have six words carried such potential for peril. Too many investors choose the worst possible times to get into a stock: They're so anxious to get on board that they feel they need to do it immediately.

That kind of anxiousness happens a lot with initial public offerings (IPOs). Palm is the perfect example. The day of Palm's IPO, the stock debuted at $38 per share. It topped out at a sky-high $165, and then eventually collapsed.

Why did that happen? Unlike most high-tech companies, Palm was familiar to the general public. Lots of people owned Palms and trusted the brand. Based on this consumer confidence and not much else, many investors put in market orders for the Palm IPO. They empowered their brokers or online services to buy shares as soon as they became available, whatever the price, because they wanted in.

All of this hastiness drove the stock up tremendously within the first few hours it was available. At that point, despite the excitement, Palm wasn't worth its post-IPO price tag. I was pretty sure it would come down.

The reason for my feeling was 3Com. 3Com owned nearly 100 percent of Palm on the day Palm went public, but despite that fact, the Street didn't value 3Com as highly as Palm. This had next to nothing to do with the actual value of the two companies, and almost everything to do with the fact that so many people were anxious to buy Palm and willing to buy it at any price.

Hastiness drove Palm's share price up, but those who were hasty to buy Palm's stock lost out. The smart investors sold to them. The smart investors had done their homework, and they bought 3Com prior to the Palm IPO (or sold Palm shares acquired at the IPO price for a huge gain), because owning 3Com meant you owned Palm at a much lower price.

OMISSION

Omission is when you have deep knowledge concerning the worth of a stock and you don't act upon it. This sin irks me to no end. I can't understand why someone with a huge advantage in a certain area would choose to invest blindly in another one instead. But for whatever reason, it happens all the time.

For example, I have a number of friends who are doctors. All they want to buy is tech stocks. A few years ago, I was at dinner with one of these friends, who was bemoaning the fact that HMOs were taking over his practice. "There's no way a little guy like me can beat them," he said. "They're just too big." The game, in his opinion, was over. Did he invest in one of these companies, instead of just complain about them? Nope.

Another doctor friend kept raving to me about a new drug he was convinced would change the world. But he didn't invest in the drug company. Instead, he bought shares in Peapod, an online grocery store whose shares have since plummeted from $15.50 to $2.75.

I, too, have fallen prey to the sin of omission. My biggest mistake ever wasn't in the high-tech arena, it was in drink. The nectar of the gods, to be exact—coffee.

Now, I'll be honest: I'm a coffee fanatic—some might even say an addict—so while I'm not in the coffee business, I know a lot about the bean. Having traveled extensively in Europe for business and frequented many a coffeehouse over the years, I was witness more than a decade ago to a European phenomenon that had yet to hit the States: Coffee drinking as event.

I saw that the European coffee culture was as much about the atmosphere as it was about the brew, and I recognized that people were willing to pay a lot more for a cup of joe if it was in the right environment.

About 10 years ago, I started doing a lot of business in Seattle, and I noticed this little company called Starbucks that was starting to appear on a number of street corners. I watched people go in and pay $2 or $3 for a latte or a cappuccino, and a light bulb went on in my head: This company was bringing what I'd seen in Europe stateside. After a few days spent in Seattle and many an hour spent in Starbucks, it was pretty obvious to me that the company was onto something huge—and I knew all about it, early on.

Did I run the numbers and invest in the company? Nope. Somehow, I managed never to do the work, never to follow up, never to buy the stock.

Danielle refers to sins of omission as "the ones that got away," and she has her own regrets—eBay, for one. A friend of hers told her all about it in 1997, after he'd bid on a hard-to-find watch and snagged it for $50. Danielle tried eBay out and recognized its potential long before the stock shot up into the ether. She even bid on something. Did she buy the stock? No. Nor did she buy Ask Jeeves, a search engine she used to write her first book and had described prebuzz as "The best thing to hit the Web, ever." Heartbreaking.

Arrogance

The sin of arrogance is a different beast entirely. It occurs when you take yourself so seriously that you think you know more than you do, so you buy without doing any computation at all. Unfortunately, overconfidence can kill you.

There's an expression that you'll often hear on Wall Street when a stock takes a nosedive: "What does the market know that I don't?"

When a stock tanks but the market as a whole stays pretty stable, there's a feeling among professional investors that some knowledge or information out there is driving the stock downward. Those of us who work on the Street try as hard as we can to understand what that knowledge is before we make a decision to buy or sell. We don't want to be so arrogant that we assume we personally know more than the market as a whole, without first checking things out, and neither should you.

When Wall Street starts getting skittish about a stock it formerly loved, there's usually a good reason. Take Netscape, for example. The company was a Wall Street darling from the time it went public until late 1995. Suddenly, the stock began to lose momentum. This falloff was a direct result of rumors that Microsoft was getting its act together in the browser space. Soon afterward, Microsoft officially announced its Internet strategy at a meeting held for analysts and the press.

Investors who were arrogant ignored Netscape's yo-yo performance and didn't investigate. More prudent Investors combed the press to uncover the reasons behind the stock's erratic performance, thereby saving themselves from purchasing a formerly hot property with a new cloud hanging over its head.

Knowing the reason behind a stock's erratic performance (whether it has shot upward or downward) is the only way to make an informed decision. Once you know the reason, you can choose to agree or disagree with the consensus.

For example, at this writing, Microsoft stock is trading extremely low ($64 per share) because of the Department of Justice (DOJ) lawsuit. It's my belief that this is overly low. I don't think things will turn out as badly for the company as they look at this particular moment.

Judge Jackson has just ruled in favor of the DOJ's suggestion that the company be broken up. But if I were a gambler, I'd place the odds that it *won't* be broken up at 2 to 1. And even if it *is* broken up, my analysis indicates that, like AT&T, the parts will be worth even more than the whole. I've put my money where my mouth is by going on the record with *Fortune,* the *New York Times,* CNBC, and others. But I stand virtually alone.

My opinion is based on knowledge, not arrogance. I know what has driven the stock down, but I've done my homework. I've examined antitrust laws and spoken to antitrust experts. I've pored over other DOJ lawsuits, and I've evaluated the situation in all its complexity. I know why Microsoft stock is in the doghouse, but I don't agree with the general consensus. In fact, I think its a great time to buy.

NEGLIGENCE

What do I mean by negligence? I mean that most people simply don't check the facts—not out of arrogance, out of laziness.

Let's take MP3.com as an example. Here's a stock that did quite well for awhile. The problem for many of its investors, though, is that they bought the stock without doing any digging.

And because of that, they didn't know that the company had a copyright lawsuit pending against it. This information was readily available to anyone who bothered to look.

The smart investor factored in the risk. The negligent one was unaware of the problem. And the company's problem became the negligent investor's problem. MP3.com lost the lawsuit, and the stock went down by more than 50 percent.

SUBMISSIVENESS

This sin doesn't take a lot of explanation. It's just as it appears—someone tells you how to invest, and you agree blindly. Maybe it's your broker, maybe it's your mother. Who knows? But no matter how smart your source is, following *anyone's* advice without doing the work yourself can only lead to trouble.

Your broker may be smart. Your broker may be nice. But basically, your broker gets paid a commission every time you buy or sell a stock. Your broker has a compelling reason to push things at you. And your broker's firm has a compelling reason to provide him or her with a list of stocks to push. I have many friends who've lost their shirts by submitting to their broker's advice.

Now I'm not saying you should stop your ears up with cotton. By all means, listen to your experts, and pick their brains for some candidates to try out, but then use the methods in this book to analyze those companies on your own. No broker is omnipotent, and even your mother doesn't know everything.

LETHARGY

There was a point a few years ago when the market cracked and stocks took a beating. This made a lot of people nervous, but for the informed investor, it was a golden opportunity. The only thing standing in the way of netting a bargain was lethargy.

I fell prey to it myself. I wanted to buy Cisco. I knew it was a great stock. In fact, I already had some, but I wanted to double my position. I also wanted to buy America Online (AOL). I never did—lethargy at its worst.

I knew the time was ripe. I knew the companies were gems and the shares were undervalued, but I was busy. I just didn't get around to putting in the order. Because of lethargy, I missed the window. I then had to grin and bear it as I watched both stocks triple within a few short months.

As an investor, you should be prepared in advance of events to jump on an opportunity when it arises. For every stock in your current portfolio, and for every stock you're considering, you should maintain up-to-date information on expected earnings, appropriate P/Es, and anticipated growth. When the market in general, or one of your stocks in particular, drops precipitously, be ready to pounce. Use the homework you've done with this book and take advantage of unusual turns in the market. If any of your stocks are trading at a price you've determined to be a bargain, don't let laziness get the better of you.

It's important to buy on the dips. Resisting lethargy and acting quickly can have a huge impact on your portfolio's performance.

GREED

You've got a stock that's shooting through the roof. It has performed better than you ever thought it could in your wildest dreams. At some point, you've got to admit that it's overvalued.

But despite your golden child's performance, you're greedy. Maybe it will keep going up, you think. You decide to take your chances.

May 2000 brought a lot of pain to a lot of greedy people. The bottom fell out from under the market, and at this writing, we are still seeing the fallout.

In the euphoria of a strong economy during the late 1990s, many investors bought stock in companies they knew next to nothing about. The lucky ones watched their stocks rise in an almost irrationally bullish market. But even after they'd made a mint, most didn't sell. Plus, they never sat down and figured out what the stocks were actually worth. They just assumed that there was no end in sight. Because they were too greedy to take their profits and leave the casino, they paid dearly.

SUMMING UP

- Too many investors purchase stocks blindly. Knowledge is the key to success in the stock market.
- Avoid investing's Seven Deadly Sins:
    1. Don't be so anxious to buy a stock that you buy at any cost.
    2. Invest in what you know.
    3. Never assume you know more than the Street.
    4. Don't let laziness get the better of you—do your homework.
    5. Don't follow tips or advice blindly.
    6. Be prepared in advance—then you can pounce when opportunity arises.
    7. When a stock you own is sky high, don't assume there's no end in sight.

Thomas G. Kamp is a portfolio manager for Alliance Capital's Large Capitalization Growth Group, which has $85 billion of the $388 billion in assets managed by Alliance as a whole. He was recently voted Fund Manager of the Year by the *South China Morning Post* for having the best three- and five-year performance in the (offshore) U.S. Equity category. The American Growth Portfolio that he manages was named the 1999 Benchmark Fund of the Year by *Benchmark* magazine.

What was the best stock you ever bought?
Why was it attractive to you at the time?

My fund has had many great stocks. But I think one of the more interesting stories is that of our investment in Motorola in early 1993.

Motorola was beginning to get a lot of attention in the early 1990s as cellular telephone usage began to take off. Then, in January 1993, ABC's *20/20* aired a segment about the allegation that cellular phones cause brain cancer. Even before this segment aired, as rumors of the negative piece began to circulate on Wall Street, Motorola's stock price started to drop. Prior to this, Motorola's stock price had been in the high $60s. The morning after the television program, the stock opened at $49 per share . . . with our purchases.

We stepped up to purchase Motorola in large size because we had a lot of data indicating that the company was a sound investment. We'd followed the company for some time and had done our homework on the fundamentals. Motorola was well positioned in each of the different wireless technologies that were being developed at that time: paging, analog cellular, specialized mobile radio (IDEN), and even satellite (Iridium).

Furthermore, I knew that Motorola had tested cellular phones at 10 times their normal transmitting power on a large group of pigs for 30 days at 24 hours per day. They'd then killed the pigs and dissected their brains looking for any nonnormal cell growth. I knew that they'd found nothing. Motorola probably just didn't want to talk about it for fear of animal rights activists.

Let me tell you something. There are a lot of very bright, hardworking people in this industry. But the key point here is that investing success is not the result of being smarter than everyone else. Rather, the key is to get lots of data points "up on the wall." It is those investors with the most data that will have the clearest picture of reality. Then it takes the courage of conviction to bet against the crowd in moments of great uncertainty.

What was the worst stock you ever bought?
What were your miscalculations?

The stock that had the greatest negative impact on our client's portfolios was Applied Materials, back in 1995. Our mistake was believing comments from Texas Instruments' economist, Vladi Cato, that semiconductors were achieving such omnipresence that the industry was becoming less cyclical. We observed the explosive demand growth in the sector, and we became one of Applied Materials' largest shareholders. We then proceeded to ride the stock over the top (post–August 1995) as the cycle matured and new semiconductor equipment orders evaporated.

The mistake we made was that we failed to appreciate the concentration of orders coming from the DRAM manufacturers—which represented over 40 percent of the semiconductor equipment industry's orders. The DRAM industry enjoyed three years of above-trend-line pricing because demand far outstripped supply. But when supply finally began to catch up with demand, orders for new equipment (which Applied Materials supplied) began to evaporate, even though numerous fabrication facilities were already under construction. Applied Materials stock began to nosedive. It ultimately lost 60 percent of its value from the peak in August 1995.

I'll never forget a meeting I had with the management of Applied Materials in the late summer of 1995, right near the peak. I asked the treasurer, Nancy Handel, about recent order activity, and she was visibly nervous in her vague response. Unfortunately, we met with a lot of people that day who exuded confidence and we did not sell. In hindsight, I made a significant mistake by not taking her nervousness as a sign that orders were in jeopardy of being canceled. Her attitude was an important data point, and I should have paid more attention to it.

CHAPTER FIVE

INVEST IN GREAT MANAGEMENT

I remember when I first heard about Amazon.com. My company was taking Amazon public, and I went out to dinner with the analyst handling the deal on the night of the big debut. He was distraught.

I asked him what was upsetting him, and he almost couldn't get the words out. "Mike," he said, "they were supposed to price the shares at $17 each and the bankers upped it to $18 a share without telling me!"

He looked so upset, I tried my best not to smile. "Look," I said, "in a year's time, Amazon is either going to be worth a hundred dollars a share, or zero. Either way, no one's going to remember the dollar."*

At that time, e-commerce was relatively new. It was May 1997, and people were still mostly using the Web as a search tool. It was clear that Amazon had a *shot* at a major breakthrough, but the general consensus was that if Barnes & Noble decided to make a Web play, Amazon would be crushed underfoot. With the threat of

---

*Ironically enough, it was this very analyst's work that had convinced me that Amazon had a competitive advantage over brick-and-mortar book-sellers and would turn out to be huge. After reading his analysis, it was clear that $1 was meaningless—maybe *$100* would matter, but not $1.

Barnes & Noble lurking in people's minds, there was a lot of fear among investors.

The good news was that my company had a secret weapon: Jeff Bezos. The moment I heard Jeff speak for the first time, I knew that anyone who listened to him would be soothed on the spot. The guy was whip smart.

But more than smarts, Jeff had the one thing I look for in any great chief executive officer (CEO)—*paranoia*. He saw the risks; he knew the challenges ahead; and he was ready to admit them, talk about them, and face them head on. In the relatively new world of e-commerce, he understood what most others didn't—the Web was a brand game. It might be a level playing field for anyone who wanted to get in on the ground floor, but it would be branded quickly, and whoever got to the brands first would be almost impossible to unseat.

Ted Waitt, the founder of Gateway Computer, is another prime example of managerial gold. I knew it from the moment I met him—despite meeting him in a somewhat strange location. My first official meeting with Ted Waitt was in 1991, walking through a cow pasture in the pouring rain. Gateway wasn't a public company yet, and the pasture doubled as the company parking lot. Headquarters was located next to the cows, in a prefab metal building. Despite the smell, I was already impressed—the company certainly wasn't squandering finances on accommodations.

After spending two hours with Ted Waitt, it was obvious that behind his bohemian demeanor was one of the best brains in the industry. He might have been young, but he was anything but naive. He had negotiated incredible prices on components; he'd mastered the art of shipping things cheaply; he'd even finagled a deal with a community in South Dakota for land, so that his facilities would cost less than anyone else's in the business.

However, all of this paled in comparison to his grasp of marketing. Ted identified his ideal customers and went after them with a vengeance. Because of this, Gateway positioned itself perfectly—as a unique company making machines for unique people. Gateway's sometimes campy but always hip ads solidified its image, and great products and unparalleled customer support and service made first-time customers into lifetime customers.

When I first met Ted, Gateway was a small company, but after meeting him, I knew that it was going to be huge. I identified Gateway as one of the five key players in the PC industry long before it was a household name. Seven years later, it became the number-one consumer PC company in America.

Let me let you in on a little secret: In the world of high tech, having the best technology is not enough. A high-tech business, just like any other business, is only as strong as the people who run it. Regardless of a company's potential, or a product's inherent superiority, the quality of company management should be the number-one factor in making your investment decision about any company in any industry. Trust me, I learned this lesson the hard way (see box).

WHAT TO LOOK FOR

Two of the smartest portfolio managers I know—Scott Schoelzel, of the Janus Twenty Fund (the best-performing large-cap fund of 1998), and Fred Kobrick, who *Money* magazine called "one of the top five portfolio managers of the decade"—believe so strongly in the importance of management that they insist on meeting with the top managers of a company before investing a dime.

If you have the time and the ability to meet management in person, by all means, do it. But mostly you won't have this luxury. You'll have to rely on shareholder's meetings, television appearances, newspaper or magazine articles, and the like.

This chapter describes what to look for in a management team. It explains four factors I like to see in a company and why. Keep in mind, these are the things that I *ideally* like to see. Just because a company violates a rule doesn't mean it's destined for failure.

WHAT MIKE LIKES

- The founder of the company still works there and is under 50 years old.
- The founder off-loads the running of the company to someone else.
- The management team keeps a cool head in times of crisis and isn't afraid to bring in an outsider to fix things.
- The company takes hiring extremely seriously. Management gets the best people and does whatever is necessary to keep them sharp and satisfied.

LEARN FROM MY MISTAKES

It's easy to write about success. I've been involved in my share of it in this industry. I could restrict things to the wins—after all, it's my book! But I think it's instructive for people to understand that no matter how successful any investor (professional or not) is, there are plenty of failures along the way.

I made one of my biggest mistakes in the middle of a hot streak. As I mentioned in the introduction, my forecasts on Microsoft tossed me into the limelight as an analyst somewhat early on. I developed a bit of a following. Soon after Microsoft, I picked my next stock darling—Borland. It's hard to believe now, but as big as Microsoft was, Borland started out even bigger.

It all began with a recommendation to buy, which I placed on the stock at around $20 a share. The stock shot up to $85 a share in a very short time, maybe a year. As the stock catapulted toward that $85 mark, it became somewhat obvious that it had gotten a little ahead of itself. It was overvalued.

The interesting thing was that as Borland climbed closer to $85 per share, more and more analysts started to recommend it. Most analysts jumped aboard the recommendation bandwagon when the stock was between 70 and 85.

At the height of the fever, I started to get a little bit nervous. I thought about downgrading Borland from a buy to a hold. Even if things played out as I hoped, it seemed that the valuation was getting a little rich. I won't try to claim that I had any idea at the time that Borland would run into trouble, because I didn't, but the stock did appear overvalued.

I brought my doubts to a veteran analyst at my firm who said, "We downgraded Wal-Mart, because of similar thinking, before it had run all the way up, and that was the worst mistake we ever made." As I said, I was the new guy on the block. And listening to this, I thought, "Wow. I don't want to be the guy who downgraded Wal-Mart." I held firm.

The Wal-Mart story made me hesitate, but it wasn't the only reason I didn't pull out of the stock. The second reason, which is almost embarrassing to admit, was that my report, the culmination of months of research and analysis, hadn't come out yet. And I thought, "How can I downgrade Borland when the report is coming out next week?" The third thing stopping me was that I hadn't yet found out if my thinking was right. The reason the stock had gone up was because people *believed* I was right in my analysis of Borland—that once the company shipped its new Windows versions, it would gain more market share. But not enough time had passed to determine for certain whether my predictions were valid.

For me, the whole Borland frenzy culminated at an analyst's meeting at Borland's headquarters, in October 1991. Borland was showing the Windows versions of its Quattro Pro spreadsheet, its new (dBase) database, and its traditional database, Paradox. After the demonstration, the Borland people told us that all four products would ship sometime between January and March 1992.

The room started buzzing. It appeared to a lot of us analysts that once Borland shipped these Window versions of its products, the company would be hard to stop. Paradox was sailing along, and Borland had just acquired Ashton Tate (and, thereby, dBase), so now the company had the two dominant products in the database arena. Quattro Pro was no slouch—it was already taking market share away from Lotus 1-2-3 on the DOS platform. With the announcement that Windows versions were almost ready to be shipped, success seemed assured. The room was in an uproar.

After the meeting, a bunch of analysts got to talking. There was a feeling of frenzy in the air. All around me, people were whipping out their phones and calling in estimates for Borland's next fiscal year. I overheard an analyst say her earnings estimate was $3.00 per share. A few minutes later, someone told her that I was at $4.00 per share. She went to the phone immediately and called in a new estimate of $4.00. The bumps fed upon each other. In the few minutes we were sitting there, the stock shot up several more points.

(Continued)

As I said, the room was buzzing. Even with expectations high, it looked like an easy win for Borland. All the company had to do was ship its products when it said it was going to ship them. It was a shoo-in situation.

And now we come to why this interlude is attached to the chapter on management. Execution and the ability to execute are as critical as or more critical than any other thing you evaluate in a company. Failure to execute is what brought the Borland house of cards crashing down.

What happened? Nothing drastic. Borland failed to get the Windows versions of its products out when promised. In the interim, Lotus shipped a Windows version of its competing product, 1-2-3. In an odd stroke of luck for Borland and its product Quattro Pro, Lotus's new version of 1-2-3 was defective. Had Borland shipped Windows versions *then*, it still could have won the game.

Unfortunately, Borland's management continued to drag its heels. Tired of waiting, with Lotus 1-2-3 not working properly and Borland's spreadsheet software not even on the shelves, many Windows customers decided to try out a product that was an underdog at the time—Microsoft Excel—mostly because they had no other choice.

Borland's tardiness cost it momentum, just as more and more customers were migrating to the Windows platform. At this critical time, Borland stopped gaining market share and started losing it. Plus, the severe delays in release caused another problem: While Borland's products were being held up, new features were being added to competing products. Borland's worries about the need to add these features to its own spreadsheet delayed shipping even further. Risky marketing and distribution decisions added to the downward spiral.

Once the stock started coming down, I made the mistake of thinking "Well, it's much cheaper now. How can I downgrade it with those new products right around the corner?" So I stayed with the stock way too long and caused a lot of damage to my career. Some of the portfolio managers who had come to the stock late, when it had already been run up, and had lis-

tened to me and stayed with it on the way down, lost a significant amount of money.

Because I'd been so closely associated with the rise of Borland, I was also closely associated with the fall of Borland. I
eventually bounced back, and so did my clients, but the Borland fiasco taught me a valuable lesson: No matter how great a
company is, and no matter how great its product, I will never
again rate a stock a buy if the management team isn't
absolutely top-notch.

HAIL THE FOUNDER

I think it's a good sign when the founder of a company is still
working there. All too often, when you get into second- or third-
generation management, business takes a downward turn. Re-
placement leaders may have their MBAs, and they may be very
experienced managers, but they are usually not visionaries.

I like it when the founder remains at the helm because he or
she has a vested interest in the company doing well over the long
haul; quite often, said founder has a very large chunk of stock and
a personal identification intricately linked to the company. In contrast, professional managers aren't usually vested in a company
doing well forever; they often manage for the short term because
they are rewarded for short-term gains.

I've set an arbitrary rule that the founders of all of your companies should not only be at the helm, but under age 50. Please
keep in mind that this doesn't mean that you sell the stock the day
your favorite CEO turns 50. If you're still comfortable with the way
things are running, hold on to it.

However, when you're *initially* looking at investing in a company, look for young CEOs. I want you to find companies you can
stay with for five years or more. Technology changes in the blink of
an eye—it's good to have a relatively young and extremely flexible
person running things. For the majority of high-tech companies,
this won't even be an issue—most founders in high tech have
barely reached their thirtieth birthdays.

Don't get me wrong—I'm no ageist. In fact, I'm over 50 myself. But technology is a very fast paced business. And while age shows a certain amount of maturity and experience, I've found that a lot of CEOs begin to falter once they hit a certain benchmark. They get out of touch with where the industry is going.

Take Digital Equipment. The company's founder, Ken Olsen, was one of the smartest people in the entire industry—but at a certain point, he lost track of where the market was heading. The PC revolution swept in and Olsen ignored it. Not only did he ignore it, but he was extremely antagonistic toward the new technology. Maybe it was his background in minicomputers. Maybe it was because of his age. Either way, his resistance to change hurt his company tremendously.

Ray Noorda, the CEO of Novell, was sharp as a tack until about age 60, at which time he started to forget things. On numerous occasions I watched him completely lose his train of thought in the middle of answering an interview question. It was obvious to anyone who knew Noorda in his heyday that he wasn't as strong as he'd been before—and it was obvious that with Noorda at the helm, the company was in trouble.

HELP WANTED

Youth and ambition are wonderful qualities in a high-tech CEO. But once the company reaches a certain size, founders should be willing to bring in someone else to run it. What makes a Bill Gates, or a Michael Dell, or a Jeff Bezos a force to reckon with is their vision, not their accounting prowess. I'm partial to founders who give themselves the freedom to lead the company into the future, by ignoring day-to-day operations and focusing their attention on the big things: strategy, product, and relationships.

Unlike some of his counterparts in the business, Michael Dell, CEO of Dell Computer Corporation, grasped this concept early on. He knew that running operations was a waste of his energies, so he turned administration over to an expert administrator and liberated himself from operational responsibility. Mort Topfer was brought in from Motorola to be Dell's chief operating officer (COO), and Tom

Meredith from Sun Microsystems stepped in as Dell's chief financial officer (CFO). They achieved what Michael Dell himself had not.

Tom Meredith turned Dell Computer around by tightening controls over inventory and accounts receivable, which cut costs and made Dell run much more smoothly. Meredith asked suppliers to put miniwarehouses near Dell's manufacturing plants so that inventory could be more rapidly restocked. The result was *just-in-time inventory management*—inventory needs were estimated ahead of time, and goods didn't sit in the warehouse waiting to be used.

Today, Dell has taken the concept one step further: The company's newest warehouses require no storage at all. Trucks pull up, goods are picked directly off the back, and manufacturing begins immediately.

Mort Topfer made his mark at Dell by launching a new strategic planning process. Topfer introduced *rolling five-year forecasting*, which forced managers to think about what their hiring, strategic, and facility needs would be over the next five years and to begin planning how they would fill those needs well before they had to face them in earnest.

By hiring Topfer and Meredith to run operations, Michael Dell provided himself with the freedom to guide the overall vision of the company. Dell had the good sense not to waste his time and talents on work better done by an administrator.

And speaking of good sense, regardless of my long-standing disapproval of Apple over the years, I have to give Steve Jobs credit for putting a master marketer on the job early on—John Sculley. Sculley was brought in to allow Jobs to off-load some of his responsibilities and concentrate on Apple's future. Unfortunately, a few years later Sculley organized a palace coup and kicked Jobs out of the company.

Losing Jobs was the beginning of the end for Apple. Just as a visionary shouldn't run administration, an administrator shouldn't be in charge of vision. Sculley was a fantastic marketer, but he was a *soda* guy. He came from Pepsi.

After Jobs was gone and a little time had passed, Sculley made himself chief *technology* officer. If you needed to know about soft drinks, Sculley was your man, but he knew nothing about technology. The minute I heard him speak on technology, I told people to sell their shares in Apple; so did most analysts. Sculley was clueless.

For the next six and a half years, I had a negative call on Apple. The 1990s were a golden age for most hardware companies. While Dell's stock was appreciating more than a hundred-fold, Compaq more than thirtyfold, and almost every other major PC company was shooting through the roof, Apple's stock actually declined—from $48 a share to $40.

Apple had the best products on the market, but as I mentioned before, technology isn't enough. It's next to impossible for a company to soar with a managerial albatross hanging from its neck. Under Sculley, Apple got everything wrong. Its strategy was misplaced, its products were too expensive to build, and its management team didn't know how to run the company. It was only at the beginning of 1999 that things started to turn around. Jobs returned, and with good management in place again, Apple started to come back from the dead.

Observing a company in hot water

Have you ever heard the phrase, "The first step to recovering from a drug problem is admitting that you have one"? Well, I would argue that this is the first step to recovering from *any* problem. When you're considering investing in a company, it's important to look at its track record. Look hard. Ask yourself: How does this management team react to crisis?

Hopefully, not like IBM. At IBM, politics often outweigh good sense. Consider IBM's situation in 1988: The company was floundering. Profits were down and costs were sky high. It became evident that the company would have to let some people go in order to survive. The problem was that IBM didn't want to *say* that it was letting people go. For some reason, that was very important to IBM—not to say it.

Instead of admitting that it had a problem, IBM came up with a plan: The company would offer every single employee voluntary retirement, rather than laying anyone off. Give people several years salary, an acceleration of their pension plans, and other perks, and IBM figured enough employees would leave of their own accord. The company wouldn't have to fire a soul.

The plan landed on the desk of a top IBM manager I know very well. He was horrified. The manager went to John Akers, the CEO, and said, "I think it's a very bad idea to make this available to everybody. We're going to lose our best people." Akers disagreed. The good people, in Akers's opinion, would never leave.

Well, the announcement was made and who do you think took the offer—the employees who could get another job in a heartbeat, or the people who'd been struggling to appear useful for years? Take a wild guess. Over 80 percent of the people who took IBM up on voluntary retirement were among the highest-rated employees the company had. IBM lost a whole layer of terrific management, because when crisis hit, it was too embarrassed to admit that it was letting people go.

BRING IN AN EXPERT

The companies I respect most aren't afraid to admit they have a problem. They're not afraid to bring in an expert to fix the area in which they're falling short. I see this as a sign of strength, not weakness.

Take, for example, Michael Kinsley, editor of the high-profile political Web magazine, *Slate,* whisked away when Microsoft needed help in the new media arena, or Jim Allchin, the designer of Banyon's networking operating system, brought on board when Novell was killing Microsoft in networking. Trouble with the next-generation operating system? No problem. Microsoft hired David Cutler and a dozen of his VMS design team members from Digital Equipment, the leading competition. From Mike Maples, brought in from IBM to lend some much-needed structure, to Jon Shirley and Bob Herbold, operations gurus from Radio Shack and Procter & Gamble, Microsoft has never been afraid of bringing in seasoned veterans from the outside to help turn things around. Not only does recruiting top executives from other companies help Microsoft by infusing management with outside expertise, but it also weakens the competition by removing key leadership.

By bringing in a veteran like Bob Herbold, Microsoft, then a relatively immature company, was able to benefit from Herbold's years of experience at powerhouse Procter & Gamble. Before Herbold's arrival, Microsoft was determined to do everything in-house. For example, when it needed an internal information system to manage its accounting, rather than outsourcing the job to an expert, Microsoft programmers were asked to write a program from scratch.

Herbold changed all that. He realized that it was ridiculous to have Microsoft's programmers spend thousands of hours creating a system outside their realm of expertise, rather than buy a system from a specialist. He decided to hire SAP, the number-one vendor in enterprise management systems, to design a system for Microsoft, using NT Server.

In addition to saving Microsoft money, the outsourcing had an unexpected benefit. Microsoft had been trying to convince the business world that its NT Server operating system, meant to compete with Unix, was powerful enough to run a multi-billion-dollar company. It was a hard sell. While most customers believed NT Server could run management software for a small company, the general feeling was that the big guys would be better off with a Unix or minicomputer system. By hiring SAP to create Microsoft's enterprise management system on NT Server, Microsoft served as its own test case, demonstrating NT's power beyond a doubt. The project enhanced Microsoft's relationship with SAP and encouraged SAP to upgrade its commitment to designing for the NT system.

Thanks to Herbold, Microsoft has embraced outsourcing in other areas as well. The move has resulted in streamlined operations, reduced cost of goods, cheaper operating costs, and enhanced profits.

Like Microsoft, Dell Computer has benefited from a bit of managerial poaching in times of trouble. When Michael Dell found his company floundering in notebook computers, he evaluated the competition and identified Apple's newly released Power-Books as the best-designed products in the laptop category. Dell then recruited about a dozen of the top people from Apple's PowerBook team, including the lead designer, John Medica, to create a new Dell laptop.

The overhaul cost Dell dearly in the near term. Medica's team viewed Dell's old laptops as unmarketable, resulting in the cancellation of all existing notebook projects. The long term was a different story entirely. About 18 months after the overhaul, Dell launched its first highly successful notebook series, which has been gaining significant market share ever since. Michael Dell later replicated the strategy in servers, with equally startling success.

On the flip side, there was IBM. When the PC revolution hit, IBM blundered. IBM was a mainframe company, and its management just didn't get it with PCs. And no wonder—they had a mainframe guy running their PC division. He failed. Guess what they did? They hired another mainframe guy. And when that guy failed, they hired *another* mainframe person. He failed, and they hired still another one. Eventually, IBM put someone with a nonmainframe background in charge of PCs. He was from a cookie company.

While this fiasco was unfolding, during the late 1980s and early 1990s, I was blasting IBM in my coverage as an analyst. I happened to know a portfolio manager who was one of IBM's biggest shareholders. His fund had so many shares of IBM that the CEO of the company met with this guy *directly*, one on one.

One day the shareholder came to me and said, "Mike, you keep blasting IBM. I know you think they're doing a horrible job of running their business. I'm meeting with John Akers, the CEO, in a few days. What should I tell him he needs to do to improve things?"

I just shook my head. "Look," I said, "it's so simple. But I guarantee you Akers won't do it." The guy got excited. I mean, he had millions of shares in IBM. He was dying to know what the "simple" thing was. I told him: "What IBM should do is buy this very little company called Dell and turn IBM's entire PC business over to Michael Dell, its founder."

Now you've got to understand, Dell Computer was practically a gnat at the time. It had only about a $500 million market cap; IBM had something like a $100 billion. It would have been a very small acquisition for IBM, and Michael Dell was a PC genius. I told the shareholder that if IBM put Michael Dell in charge of its PC division and put IBM's assets at his disposal, it would dominate the PC industry within a few short years.

Well, to make a long story longer, the shareholder went into his meeting with Akers. Needless to say, he was practically laughed out of the office. There was no way IBM was going to turn its PC business over to a kid. (Dell was 27 at the time.)

The rest is history. If IBM had been willing to swallow its pride and utilize Dell's passion and knowledge of PCs, it could have led the PC gold rush. But it was too stubborn to admit that it needed an outsider, especially such a young one from such a small company. That was in 1992. Today Dell Computer Corporation, the former gnat, has a market cap that's almost equal to IBM's.

COMPAQ

While IBM was making a mess of things, Compaq wasn't doing too well, either. The company only had about 4 to 5 percent of the American PC market, and instead of increasing, its share was starting to level off. Because Compaq was doing really well *outside* the United States, the slowdown was somewhat obscured. No one really knew that Compaq was in trouble.

It wasn't an analyst who figured it out—it was Ben Rosen, who had backed Compaq financially in the beginning and was now chairman of the board. Rosen watched the industry religiously, and he saw that other companies, like Gateway, were making more profit per computer than Compaq, even though Compaq had greater buying power, better engineering, lower royalties, and a higher price per machine. He realized that something was very wrong.

Rosen didn't know what that something was, but he decided to find out. He started what's referred to in the industry as a *skunkworks* project. (A skunkworks is a secret assignment, outside of normal company operations, led by a few hand-picked employees.) Rosen assembled a team of engineers and asked them to build a computer comparable to a Compaq machine, but to build it completely from industry-standard parts.

The Compaq skunkworks operation project wasn't known to anyone. Even the CEO was kept in the dark. After a few months, Rosen's team completed its assignment, and one thing became blindingly clear: Compaq was in trouble. Not only had the skunkworks team been able to build a Compaq-like machine, but it had done so with off-the-shelf parts, with no buying power whatsoever, for much less than what it cost Compaq to build a comparable unit. The CEO was fired.

SELLING TO GRANDPA

The problems at Compaq and IBM were different, but their root was the same: Both companies were living in the past. Compaq and IBM had been big players in the 1980s, and the two companies were operating under the misconception that the personal computer industry was driven by engineering, much as mainframes and minicomputers had been. They failed to realize that the industry had transformed itself—it was no longer driven by the best engineering, but by the best distribution and the best price points. Today's computer customer didn't need the *best* machine—he or she needed a decent machine that was affordable. The customer wanted a Saturn, but both Compaq and IBM were hell-bent on selling a Rolls-Royce.

Luckily for Compaq, it had Rosen in its court. His skunkworks project showed the company the light, and on June 15, 1992, Compaq introduced a completely new line of products. Based on industry-standard parts, with prices cut by more than 30 percent in one fell swoop, the new line shook the industry.

Instead of following suit, IBM decided to wait and see how things played out. That indecision cost it dearly. During that summer, Compaq took a huge chunk of IBM's market share and eventually passed it as the PC industry leader.

HIRING THE BEST PEOPLE, PERIOD

A good coach is an asset to any team. But if the players stink, a coach can only do so much. In the same way, while it's imperative to invest in companies with strong management, it's important to look at who they hire in general. Making good people a priority should apply up and down the line. I've observed that the best and the brightest companies focus on the quality of *all* of their employees, and do whatever is necessary to find them, court them, hire them, and retain them. Let's use Microsoft as an example.

RECRUITING THE STRONGEST PEOPLE

If you've ever seen the movie *Blue Chips,* you have much greater insight into the Microsoft hiring process than you realize. The company scours the country for potential stars, with a drive that would put any Big 10 coach to shame. Just like any good sports scout, Microsoft recruiters descend upon colleges across America, in search of the best and the brightest.

CONDUCTING THE TOUGHEST INTERVIEWS

Microsoft has developed such a strong reputation for the depth of its on-campus interviews that candidates spend considerable time studying for them. The cramming is somewhat in vain. Despite the horror stories, Microsoft is more interested in probing a candidate's ability to learn concepts in depth than in seeing how many facts a candidate has managed to memorize.

When it comes to the technical part of an interview, Microsoft doesn't care whether a candidate knows every programming trick—it's more concerned with a candidate's critical thinking capacity. The company wants to know how a candidate designs functions, creates algorithms, takes criticism, and approaches problems he or she doesn't have the tools or the knowledge to solve.

In addition to the technical portion of the interview, there are questions that have nothing to do with software design, from "Take me through your thinking process for determining how many gas stations there are in America" to "Explain the history of the desktop." Microsoft candidates are expected to think fast on their feet. They sit through a string of extremely tough interviews, fielding difficult and unlikely questions. Those sharp enough to make it through the first round are flown to Microsoft's campus for an exhausting day of questioning with employees from all areas and at all levels—sometimes even with Bill Gates himself.

SETTING THE BAR HIGH

Despite how quickly Microsoft has grown, it retains the air of a much smaller company. There are hundreds of departments and thousands of employees, but there's an overall feeling that Big Bill is watching. The feeling is valid: Gates has his eye on almost every important project, and many smaller ones. At some point during the design stage of any new software product, a meeting with Gates is scheduled. Internally, this has come to be known as the *Bill meeting*.

This is one reason why interviewees should get used to the hot seat—they'll be spending lots of time there during their Microsoft careers. Gates is notorious for his "bandwidth," his ability to absorb and understand the smallest minutia of every aspect of a software product—from the most specialized syntax shortcuts to an anticipation of developmental pitfalls.

Microsoft employees often joke about Gates's ability to come up with questions or problems no one else has yet considered. Programmers have been known to stay up for weeks at a time before a scheduled Bill meeting, in an attempt to address every question Gates could possibly throw their way, only to be inevitably stumped at the actual encounter.

Having a situation where a crackerjack design team, working nonstop for weeks on every aspect and angle of a product, can consistently be stumped by an outsider not only clearly establishes Gates's personal scope, it sets high expectations for all involved. In anticipation of Gates's questions, the team often fine-tunes the product to a level it might never have achieved otherwise.

In reality, there are limits to even Gates's omnipotence. He can't possibly have the same depth of knowledge on a particular piece of software as a brilliant software designer who has spent day and night for months studying the problem. But his image is such that employees *believe* that he does, and his ability to absorb is such that he nearly always adds value during discussions of design.

HAVING TOP MANAGEMENT DEMONSTRATE A RELENTLESS WORK ETHIC

In addition to making his presence known at meetings, Gates is famous for his proclivity for e-mail. Bill Gates is beyond prolific—he churns out stacks of e-mails daily and responds constantly to employee postings and messages on Microsoft's intranet system. It's not unusual for his correspondence to be sent at 3 A.M. There are two hidden messages here. First, if the chairman of the company, a person responsible for Microsoft's entire direction, can take the time to communicate with an employee, then management cares, is interested in setting direction, and is watching. Second, no matter who you are at Microsoft, you are expected to work whatever number of hours it takes to get the job done.

Contrast this with another technology company, Lotus, where the CEO commonly left the office around 6 P.M., appeared arrogant, had little or no involvement in design, and was completely out of touch with employees. At Microsoft, a company that sets deadlines so tight that employees are forced to essentially live at the office to meet them, the CEO's behavior is crucial. Gates demonstrates, by example, that even the most important people in the company are dedicated to getting the job done, regardless of whether they have to work day and night to do it.

MAKING EVERY EMPLOYEE AN ENTREPRENEUR

Microsoft's corporate structure has been a great contributor to its success. The company has ballooned from its humble beginnings as a small group of friends to a very large corporation with thousands of employees. And yet, Microsoft isn't run like a large company, but as a group of small entrepreneurial companies under one roof.

Microsoft's products are broken up into numerous separate projects, each assigned to a small *feature team*. For example, there's no behemoth Office team, but a series of teams, each in charge of its own very specific area. Each Softie (Microsoft employee) is responsible for solving and anticipating problems in his or her small piece of the product. This gives employees more of a sense of ownership. They can see their individual impacts on a product, even if the number of individuals working on it is quite large. For example, there are 500 people working on Office, but the employee responsible for the design of the toolbar knows that it works because of him or her.

Ownership doesn't end there. Microsoft gives employees a vested interest in seeing Microsoft succeed, by giving them vesting options. Every employee is made an entrepreneur. Microsoft's success is the employee's success. This encourages employees to learn about things outside their areas of expertise. (So the Excel programmer keeps an eye on marketing and customer service—and maybe listens to the sticking points and problems and tries to incorporate solutions into the program's updates. And the administrative assistant surfs the net with help from Explorer and MSN, taking note of any difficulties.) This encourages employees to follow the competition and focus on what may be affecting their stock. It encourages longer hours and a greater investment of energy.

SHARING THE WEALTH

With Bill Gates now the richest person in the world, one might question how much the rest of Microsoft's employees are benefiting from the fruits of their labor. In 1992, when I first started covering the company, I became curious myself, so I decided to track the success of the Microsoft Class of 1989.

When these employees were hired, most straight out of school, they were paid less than their market value in salary but were given 3,000 shares in options at a strike price of $54 a share, or $162,000 in options—a huge amount for any employee, let alone a new one fresh out of college. (To put things in perspective, when I was a managing director at PaineWebber, I was granted 5,000 shares, or $100,000 in options—one-third less, despite my age, experience, and expertise. Needless to say, expectations for PaineWebber stock appreciation fell short of those for Microsoft, causing those options to be worth proportionately less.)

It took four and a half years for the Class of 1989's options to fully vest. (After the first 18 months they got three-eighths, with another eighth every 6 months after.) As of March 2000, the stock had split seven separate times. These splits, taken together, accumulate to 72 to 1. One 1989 share is now 72 shares. This makes the original 3,000 shares in options equal to 216,000 shares today, with a strike price of $0.75 a share. Those eighty-niners with the foresight, restraint, and nerve not to exercise any of their options are now sitting on stock worth about $24 million more than the exercised price of options. (In other words, they have the option to buy

216,000 shares of stock, priced at $110 as we write, for only $0.75 per share, or $162,000 in total.) These people have been with the company just a little more than 10 years and are around 31 or 32 years old. In reality, few have held all their stock—in fact, it's probably prudent to sell some so as to diversify risk—but by my calculations, there are over 10,000 Microsoft millionaires today.

There's a joke floating around Microsoft. A Softie goes to visit a coworker and admires his couch. He says, "Man. That is a gorgeous sofa!"

His friend shakes his head sadly. "Yeah, I guess," he says. "But do you know how much that couch cost me? $100,000."

"Oh, come on," the Softie says. "It's nice, but it's not that nice."

His coworker sighs. "I sold $3,000 worth of stock to buy that couch. Since then the stock has gone up 30 times. The damn couch cost me $100,000."

Summing up

The most important ingredient for success is the strength of a company's management team. The best companies try to extend this concept to all employees by hiring and retaining the best people.

I believe companies with a top-notch employee structure adhere to the following rules:

- Keep the founder at the helm. Ideally, he or she should be under 50.
- Let an administrator run operations.
- Recruit the best people. Go outside for key people when necessary.
- Set very high expectations for all employees, starting at the top.
- Share the wealth. Make every employee an entrepreneur.

Mark Kingdon is the founder of Kingdon Capital Management Corporation, a New York–based hedge fund that has had a gross average annual
return of more than 32 percent—since 1983.

**If you had to pick just one quality imperative for a company
to succeed, what would it be? What is the most important
element a company must possess in order for you to invest
in it?**
Fortunately, you said *company* and not *stock,* which are different questions. I
look for a lot of things in a company before investing, but if forced to choose
just one, it would be management. Strong management can attract and
retain good people, identify and acquire (internally, through a joint venture, or
by outsourcing) the technology needed, and determine the best avenues of
growth. They should, by definition, be good long-term thinkers.

**Can you talk about one of your particularly successful (or
unsuccessful) recent investments?**
The best and worst investment that I made recently was a Japanese stock
called Crayfish. The company was originally financed by Hikari Tsushin, a reseller
of mobile telephone service whose explosive growth caused investors to place
a $60 billion market value on the stock, making its chairman, Yasumitsu Shigeta,
the world's fifth-richest person. We believed that Hikari's access to the capital
markets and the company's extensive distribution network would ensure the
success of Crayfish's fast-growing e-mail service. A few months after we
invested $1 million in a private placement at 4, Crayfish went public at 40 and
started trading at 160. We sold the additional Crayfish shares we received in the
initial public offering on the second day of trading, but we were locked up on
the private placement for six long months. In the interim, a slowdown in Japanese phone sales and a restatement of Hikari's earnings led to a collapse in
Hikari's stock price and the bankruptcy of several distributors. Crayfish's sales
flattened out and its stock plummeted to 8.

**What would you advise investors to do before putting their
money into the market?**
Standing on one foot, the advice I would give investors is *know yourself.* If you
don't know who you are, the stock market is an expensive place to find out.

Ask yourself some basic questions:

- Why are you investing? Fun, retirement, or opportunistically?
- What is your pain threshold?
- How much can you afford to lose? What are your plans when and if you reach that amount of losses?
- Does your portfolio have sufficient liquidity (trading volume relative to position size) to permit you to cut your losses if you choose to do so?
- Are your rate-of-return objectives realistic, given your level of experience, the time and effort you plan to devote to investing, and the underlying growth potential and valuation of the vehicle you have chosen?

Most of all, I'd tell them: Beware of simplistic formulas or slogans. Think for yourself.

CHAPTER SIX

LOOK FOR COMPANIES WITH A COMPETITIVE ADVANTAGE

Two Porsches pull up to the pump. One gets filled up with regular unleaded gas. The other gets the high-test stuff. Which driver feels more relaxed about optimum performance?

Take two runners of equal skill; give one a pair of sneakers and make the other run barefoot. Set them on the same course, for the same time, on the same day, during the same conditions. Guess who wins.

Two companies in the same industry, with similar products, are beckoning to you. What makes one a winner and drives the other into bankruptcy? The same quality that distinguished the runners and made one engine purr while the other just ran. This is competitive advantage—that little oomph that sets winners apart from their rivals.

In business, the competitive advantage comes in many forms: technological, psychological, and economic. Sometimes it has nothing to do with product and everything to do with perception. Sometimes it's the other way around. Regardless of the reasons, a competitive advantage can make all the difference between winning and losing. As an investor, you have to be on the lookout for this edge in all its shapes and forms. It can make or break a company.

THE FOUR TYPES OF COMPETITIVE ADVANTAGE

- The virtual enterprise or increasing feedback loop
- The economic advantage
- A product that can't be replicated
- The unbeatable brand

THE VIRTUAL ENTERPRISE

If you could take a time machine back to 1981 and ask everyone on Wall Street who today's high-tech winners would be, you'd be surprised. Let's say you gave them three choices—IBM, Intel, and Microsoft—and asked "Who do you think is most likely to have maintained ownership of its part of the PC space 20 years from now?" Ninety percent would have said IBM.

At that time, IBM ruled the hardware market. It had every advantage over anyone else competing in that space. Why did it fall and the other two companies prosper?

THE FALL OF IBM AND THE RISE OF MICROSOFT

IBM started on the right path; it was really the first PC company to try a horizontal approach. Before PCs, most hardware companies (like Sun, IBM, and Hewlett-Packard) did everything themselves. They designed the operating systems, the hardware, the microprocessors, and the disk drives; they even had their own memory fabs (factories). This is what's known as *vertical integration*.

When the PC revolution hit, most companies thought things would work the same way. Apple, Commodore, and almost everyone else adopted the vertical integration philosophy from the get-go.

IBM was late to the PC party. In order to catch up, it decided that instead of using vertical integration, it would try a horizontal approach and let multiple companies compete for each slice of the pie. With this new open model, a handful of companies would win out in each space—microprocessors, disk drives, operating systems, and so on. IBM would be the big kahuna that negotiated the best deals with each supplier. The model stood to save IBM some serious cash.

It was also better for the companies competing to be suppliers of software, disk drives, and so forth. Before the open model, a company had to design a different product for every single machine. This was extremely expensive, both to produce and to distribute. With the horizontal model, if a company won in a certain space—let's say the operating system (OS)—it could spread its research and development (R&D) costs over *all* hardware companies, over all machines. If there were 100 million machines with the same *open architecture* (meaning that anyone could build a PC around a standard, well-documented *reference platform*), and $500 million a year was spent on R&D for an operating system, that would be only $5 per computer. On the other hand, with the vertical model, if a company like Apple sold 1 million machines and spent just $50 million on R&D for the operating system, it would cost $50 per machine.

With the new open architecture, hardware companies could spend less money per component than they would have if they'd tried to do everything themselves. Of course, all of this was in its infancy 20 years ago. The idea of open architecture was a new one, and the PC frontier had yet to be won.

Microsoft may be a household name today, but at that time, it was a small, relatively unknown company. It entered the fray as a software provider for IBM machines, and IBM only. This monogamy was great for IBM, but not so great for Microsoft. It wanted to be the software standard. It was determined to win the operating system piece of the open architecture pie. But in order to do that, it needed multiple partners. Microsoft started playing the field.

As mentioned, the company was small. Microsoft knew that it couldn't beat the big-time competition with money or brand name or advertising, so it took another tack. The company decided to create a virtual enterprise around its operating system—to partner up with every hardware company in the industry and get its operating system on every machine.

At the beginning, this wasn't easy. Nobody knew about Microsoft, but that didn't stop the company. Microsoft realized that it had to get every single computer manufacturer on board in order to become the standard. The company cut whatever deal it needed to in order to do that. It didn't matter what price Microsoft had to offer, what deal it had to offer—the *key first step* was to become pervasive. Microsoft knew that if it could create the impression that it was the operating system on every single PC that shipped (or a very large number of them), its software would become the standard.

Apple took the opposite tack. It decided to keep the Mac operating system exclusive to its machines. This catapulted Apple's operating system to cult status, but it also relegated its products to a small corner in retail stores. Because Microsoft's operating system was bundled with virtually every PC on the market, more companies decided to develop software for it. This convinced even *more* customers to migrate to the Microsoft platform. The more customers that migrated, the more floor space was devoted to Microsoft-compatible products in the typical retail store. The more floor space that Microsoft occupied, the easier it was to convince more companies to become partners with Microsoft and develop products for its platform.

This is what I mean by a *virtual enterprise*—a club of partners built around a product. Multiple partners make a product more compelling, because they add to its value. When a customer bought a computer with a Microsoft operating system 15 years ago, there was only a limited amount of software available for it. These days, with so many partners on board, someone who buys a Windows machine knows he or she can get dozens of applications made by Microsoft, or any of hundreds of thousands of products made by other partners. Even if the products aren't as good as those made for the Mac, the sheer number of choices available is compelling. This phenomenon is known in the industry as the *increasing feedback loop*.

THE INCREASING FEEDBACK LOOP

As more people get involved in a product, it becomes more valuable, and the more valuable it becomes, the more people get involved. It's similar to the virtual enterprise, where getting more partners for a product increases the value of the product (as evidenced by the Microsoft example), which gets more people to use it, which makes it more valuable still.

Here's how the increasing feedback loop works. Let's say only two people in the world have e-mail, and you're considering getting an account. If you don't know the other two people who have it, e-mail is not all that beneficial for you. But suppose, as is the case, that there are millions of people using e-mail, and everyone you know has it. Now, getting an e-mail account is important, because it will allow you to communicate with everyone you know.

Let's use America Online (AOL) as an example. AOL offers anyone using it (or Compuserve, which it owns) as an Internet service provider a service called the Buddy List. With it, users type in the e-mail addresses of a list of friends, and AOL then notifies them whenever any of those friends are online. They can then chat online by sending instant messages back and forth.

Within the first year it was offered, the service grew so popular that many people, especially teenagers, signed up with AOL just so they could use it. As more people signed up, more and more wanted to get on. This became a huge competitive advantage for AOL.

The increasing feedback loop, like the virtual enterprise, is a self-perpetuating phenomenon—the more people that get on board, the more likely it is that others will follow. Because of this, with new technologies it's often crucial to get up to critical mass as quickly as possible, because getting the numbers up creates an advantage both for the customers and for the product.

APPLE VERSUS MICROSOFT—THE ECONOMICS

Each year, Microsoft spends about $500 million on R&D for its Windows operating system. Because 100 million people a year buy it, this R&D cost works out to about $5 per unit.

Apple typically sells about 5 million units a year. If it spent the same $500 million (which it can't, but we'll get to that later), its R&D cost would be $100 per unit. Microsoft *sells* its operating system to Compaq for approximately $50. If Apple spent the same $500 million as Microsoft on R&D, it would spend twice as much per unit as Compaq pays for Microsoft's whole operating system.

The upshot of all this is that, over time, it is virtually impossible for Apple to spend as much as Microsoft on R&D. The economics just don't work.

For a long time, Apple charged a premium for its machines in order to help float the cost of R&D for the operating system. But at a certain point Apple had to abandon that method in order to be able to compete with the PC. The fact that Microsoft can spread R&D over so many machines gives it an extreme economic advantage over Apple.

Being the brilliant marketer that he is, Steve Jobs recently figured out how to get Apple back into the game. At his direction, the company has shed many of its product lines in order to focus its attention and resources on several key areas, like graphics and education, where Apple has traditionally excelled. Jobs realized that dominating a few key areas instead of spreading Apple too thin in multiple ones will give the company a shot at an economy-of-scale advantage.

THE ECONOMIC ADVANTAGE

I issued my first report on Dell in 1992. The company was an underdog, but I liked it. I liked it a lot. Dell came into the PC industry, a realm tight with competition, and developed a totally new way of doing things.

Michael Dell's brainstorm was to boot the retail store idea entirely and sell directly to the customer. The concept was compelling. I decided to run the numbers. In 1992, I calculated that Dell's new business model gave the company a 10 percent cost advantage over its competition.

DELL'S ADVANTAGE

Dell's economic advantage had a lot to do with inventory. Because of its direct model, the Dell way of selling computers dictated maintaining only five or six weeks of inventory. In contrast, a company like Compaq sold its computers to a retailer or distributor. The retailer or distributor would typically have eight weeks of inventory on hand. Compaq itself needed to maintain five to eight weeks of inventory, too. All told, Compaq had about 15 weeks of inventory in the pipeline at any one time.

Now, consider that the cost of building a computer goes down by 30 to 35 percent a year. That's 2 to 3 percent a month. If a company, like Dell, has two months' less inventory, that's a 5 to 6 percent economic advantage over more bloated competitors. Plus, unlike hardware vendors like Compaq, Dell sells directly to the consumer. It doesn't have to pay resellers a margin on each machine. This gives Dell an extra 4 to 5% in leverage—the remaining portion of its 10 percent economic advantage.

A 10 percent competitive advantage is no small thing. When Dell was a small company, Compaq, IBM, Hewlett-Packard, and the other big boys could have tried to nip it in the bud. Greed and inertia kept them from doing so, and because of that, Dell has become dangerous to them.

A WORD ON PRICE

Most businesses are obsessed with price, but a lower price is relevant only if it reflects a true cost advantage over the competition. If your company is so well managed and efficiently run that you can keep your prices consistently lower than the competition because it *costs* you less, price can be a powerful weapon, because you have a true cost advantage. Otherwise, you'll retain new customers only over the short term, until another company comes along with a sale.

The telephone industry is a prime example. My kids are always telling me they've switched their long-distance company again. When they're with Sprint, AT&T bombards them on a weekly basis with sales calls, trying to convince them to switch. AT&T usually offers to undercut Sprint's rates by a penny a minute during certain hours. If my kids decide to switch back to AT&T, similar offers flood in from Sprint. Because they haven't been particularly impressed with either company, they blow with the wind, switching to whichever is offering the best rates that month.

The airline industry has a similar problem. So few carriers have distinguished themselves with superior service that the bulk

DON'T JUDGE A BOOK BY ITS COVER; DO JUDGE A PRODUCT BY ITS PACKAGE

During my first year on Wall Street, I was knee deep in analysis of three major computer software companies: Microsoft, Lotus, and Ashton-Tate. Each had a lot going for it, and each had its own unique set of obstacles—about which the Street could argue to no end.

While I was interested in who had the best product, who had the best management, who had the best long-term vision, and all of the other traditional measuring sticks, I also became somewhat obsessed by a far less debated issue—who had the most efficient packaging.

In early 1991, I decided to analyze how much each company was spending on boxing its software. This might seem a bit odd, but it led to some pretty telling information. What I found, after estimating the cost of every part of each company's packaging (through what's called a *bill of materials explosion*), was that Microsoft's packaging cost only $16, Lotus's was $34, and Ashton-Tate's rang in at a whopping $70 per product.

The fact that the costs differed so widely for products that should have had similar packaging not only exhibited a huge economic advantage for Microsoft but also pointed to major mismanagement, especially at Ashton-Tate. Plus, the two companies wasting money on packaging had less remaining for advertising and R&D, functions that would greatly impact future revenue. (In fact, soon after I published my analysis, Ashton-Tate's stock tanked, and the company was forced to sell itself to Borland.)

As they say, good things come in small packages, but—perhaps even more important in the competitive advantage arena—small packaging is a good thing.

of airline customers make a decision based solely on price and flight availability. Because none of the major national airlines consistently has better prices or flight schedules than its competition, virtually all customers shop around.

Companies like Southwest Airlines are an exception. Southwest has been able to corner its segment of the market because it has a true cost advantage. Because Southwest utilizes ticketless travel and unassigned seats, there is no need for computerized seating. The cost of selling physical tickets (both in materials and employees) is eliminated, and the time it takes to check someone in is reduced, so Southwest has less overhead and requires fewer employees. Even more important, the airline is able to load and unload its planes so rapidly that it gets more flights per plane per day, another boon to its bottom line.

For all of these reasons, Southwest has an inherent cost advantage, and it passes the savings on to the customers, offering fares consistently lower than the competition's. This further strengthens its foothold.

A PRODUCT THAT CAN'T BE REPLICATED

Nobody likes a copycat. The problem with business is that companies with a good idea are almost always slapped with the sincerest form of flattery. Because of this reality, one of the greatest competitive advantages a company can possess is a product or service that can't be replicated. If you uncover a company for which this is the case, take note. If there's a market for this particular offering, a nonreplicable product can mean big bucks.

When I say a product can't be replicated, what I mean is one of two things: Either it's so costly or time consuming to copy it that it doesn't make sense to try, or it literally can't be replicated, for legal reasons. The way the latter type of competitive advantage comes about is through patents, copyrights, or trademarks. New drugs, for example, are often protected for a certain period of time before any other company is allowed to horn in on things.

Drug companies aren't the only ones that have made a killing thanks to patent protection. Several high-tech companies haven't done too badly, either. Texas Instruments, for example, holds many of the original patents on computer memory chips. Believe it or not, Texas Instruments gets a royalty for almost every memory chip that hits the market. Those royalties have been a rich source of revenue for the company, and despite a plethora of lawsuits, its patents have held strong.

Gemstar is another entity that owes its bank balance to patent protection. The company's brainchild was the first electronic program guide for television. You've probably seen it; the guide is bundled with most television sets and many cable subscriptions. For each customer, Gemstar gets a kickback—a few dollars a pop. Not only does it get the royalties, but it owns the advertising space, as well.

How tight are the patents? *Very.* Microsoft recently wanted to create its own electronic program guide for WebTV and was forced to pay Gemstar royalties on it. Let me tell you, Microsoft would go to the ends of the earth to avoid paying a royalty to anyone. If it agreed to that deal, I'd bet good money that those patents were unbreakable. Anyone who knew Microsoft and was reading the progress of all this in the papers would have known the same.

One of the most famous instances of patent protection is the Intel–AMD battle. Throughout the PC revolution, Intel provided the chips that fueled most desktop computers. At a certain juncture, though, its stranglehold started making hardware vendors (like Compaq, Hewlett-Packard, and IBM) nervous. They were worried that if something went wrong at Intel, they'd have no other source for computer processors, and their bottom lines would be at risk. Under pressure from these vendors, Intel agreed to license its technology to another chip manufacturer, AMD.

Under the terms of the deal, AMD was legally allowed to make an Intel-compatible processor without doing nearly as much R&D itself. This was a huge economic advantage for AMD, but all good things must come to an end. Eventually, Intel decided that AMD wasn't pulling its share of the load and wanted to cut it out of the loop.

Lawsuits followed. Intel won. The company had legal rights to its intellectual property, and once permission was pulled, AMD was no longer privy to the specs it needed to easily replicate Intel's product.

What AMD was permitted to do, however, was what is called a *clean room* replication. The courts ruled that while AMD couldn't have access to Intel's R&D without its permission, AMD could reverse-engineer Intel's products.

Under clean room guidelines, AMD is allowed to use publicly published information (for example, how the Intel chip interacts with an operating system like Windows) and then create the product from scratch. Legally, it is not allowed to use any person who has ever worked for Intel or had access to Intel R&D; that would violate Intel's copyrights, trade secrets, or patents. Reverse engineering has allowed AMD to stay in the game, but the lag time between when Intel first creates a new chip and when AMD is finally able to get a replication on the market has hurt the company.

In technology, patents are emerging as a key weapon in the fight to remain unique and retain a stranglehold on one's piece of the market. As an investor, it's important to determine not only how good a technology is, but how easily it can be copied. Investors should determine what products a company has attempted to protect by filing patents, and also see who has licensed those technologies. When significant potential competitors license a technology, it usually means that they realize it would be far too difficult or expensive to try to replicate it.

A good example of this phenomenon is Sun's software product, Java. This product has been licensed to players as diverse as Microsoft, IBM, Apple, and Netscape. Java is a new-generation development tool for software that works across multiple platforms (like Windows, Unix, and Mac). It is also a piece of code that can be sent through the Web (or put right on the desktop) to make it possible for any machine to run an application, regardless of what operating system is on that hardware.

In short, Java is a cross-platform enabler. It functions as middleware—in other words, it sits *between* the hardware and the operating system.

COMPETITIVE ADVANTAGE: WIN, LOSE, DRAW

Win: Corning. Corning is an old-world company, formerly known for its casserole dishes, with a patented technology that suddenly has a new application. Corning holds patents and trademarks on optical fiber, which it invented in 1970. The Internet, which uses fiber as a means of transport, has opened up a whole new market for the company. Corning's sales in 1999, much owing to these patents, were $4.3 billion.

Lose: Xerox. Many of the most important technological inventions of this decade were developed at the Xerox Research Center—the mouse, the graphical user interface (GUI), Ethernet, and the laser printer. Unfortunately, Xerox didn't patent anything. These technologies have generated billions of dollars in revenue for other companies, but Xerox hasn't seen any of it.

Draw: University of Illinois. The first Web browser, Mosaic, was invented at UI and was properly protected legally. Marc Andreessen, who worked at the university as a grad student and went on to help found Netscape, lifted some of Mosaic's technology for Netscape Navigator. He had no permission from the university, and it eventually sued Netscape and won in an out-of-court settlement. The good news for the university was that the patents held; the bad news was that, unlike Netscape, it never made much money from the browser technology it had invented.

It's precisely this intermediary position that has led to trouble. Microsoft, which acquired its dominant position in the PC space through its operating systems, doesn't like having a middleman like Java in the mix. Java threatens Microsoft's power by removing the need for developers to create software solely for Windows, because software created for Java can be shared by all platforms. To combat this cross-platform colonization, Microsoft licensed Java and developed its own version of the product—one that is optimized for Windows, but doesn't work very well on other platforms. Sun's Java works on all platforms, but not optimally on any specific one. Because Microsoft's version makes Java so much smoother on Windows machines, and most PC owners use Windows, a number of software developers began creating software on Microsoft Java.

As Microsoft Java began picking up momentum, Sun threw a curveball and sued Microsoft. According to Sun, Microsoft had violated their licensing agreement by creating a version of Java that wasn't Javaesque. After a visit to the courtroom, Sun won the case. The judge agreed that the patents had been violated and ordered Microsoft to stop abusing them. At this writing, Microsoft has appealed the decision, but has also stopped selling Java tools.

THE UNBEATABLE BRAND

Few competitive advantages are as difficult to fight as a brand name. An economic advantage may be overtaken eventually, a patent may be lifted, and a virtual enterprise may be usurped, but a great brand can be sustained for years.

Take Coca-Cola. When the company came up with the motto "Always," it wasn't kidding. Coke has had a strong brand name for nearly a century.

The company was launched in 1886 when an Atlanta druggist named John S. Pemberton began whipping up Coca-Cola syrup in a 30-gallon brass kettle he hung in his backyard. He marketed the syrup as a brain and nerve tonic and sold it through a string of local drug stores. Sales averaged nine drinks per day.

While Coca-Cola's sales that first year were a slim $50, by 1915 they had risen sharply to about $50 million. By 1944, Coke syrup manufacturing reached the billion-gallon mark. Coca-Cola began modestly, but these days, most consumers wouldn't dream of buying another soda over a Coke.

What does a company do to gain such market share? Well, over the years Coca-Cola has spent a ton on advertising, and it runs good promotions—but more important, it's not greedy. Coca-Cola doesn't make it very expensive to buy its superior brand name. It never charges more than a 20 percent premium over generic soda. Because they've kept prices reasonable, Coca-Cola and the similarly run Pepsi-Cola dominate the market. The next in line isn't even close.

A brand name can do more than retain market share—it can launch new markets. This has worked for Amazon. Amazon started as an online bookseller. A few years later, it decided to spread its reach and sell much more—CDs, DVDs, videos, even electronics. Because it developed such a strong brand, it has a sea of loyal customers, already comfortable with the site.

This gives Amazon an instant customer base for any new product launch. A consumer who stops at Amazon to order a book is more likely to order a CD at the same time than to order the book and then go to another site to get the CD.

In addition to the extra revenue, Amazon gets an added bonus from branching out. It's cheaper to pick, pack, and ship a few products (a book, a CD, and a Palm Pilot, all in the same order), than it is for Amazon to ship just one. Plus, when the company advertises, it can tout all the businesses at once. This lowers the cost for each segment.

Compare this strategy to that of a company that takes out a Super Bowl ad to sell only one product. It has paid a huge premium per head, but the product focus is extremely narrow. A good chunk of the people viewing the ad will have no interest in what the company is selling, but the company has paid for every single eyeball. An Amazon ad in the same slot has a greater chance of appealing to more people because Amazon has more products. That lowers the ad expense per head.

Note: Keep in mind that a good brand isn't always enough. It gives a company an advantage, but it may not be enough of an advantage to make it a high-growth company. For example, if the soda market isn't growing that fast and Coca-Cola's share is huge but pretty stable, huge market share isn't enough. Coca-Cola will grow at the same rate as the soda market as a whole. That might be just 10 percent a year, not the 25 percent a company needs to meet the big tech score criteria.

Almost, but not quite

A competitive advantage can be a powerful weapon, but it doesn't guarantee victory. Many companies have had a huge opportunity because of one of the reasons discussed, but have blown it.

Sony

Take Sony's Betamax. Here was a product eons ahead of its time, with a patent to boot. It was a compelling technology, and it was protected, but Sony forfeited its competitive advantage because it was unwilling to leverage it by creating an increasing feedback loop. Sony refused to license Betamax to other manufacturers, which would have ensured marketwide acceptance.

A competitive technology—VHS—came in. It wasn't as good, but it was more economical. VHS launched its own feedback loop, and because of it, Betamax was displaced.

Adobe

Adobe is another company that had a piece of the competitive advantage puzzle, but failed to use it properly. The company had created a fantastic product called Adobe PostScript, a font-rendering technology that put previous incarnations to shame.

Before PostScript, fonts were created through a technology that stored a separate dot configuration for each letter, in every possible style and size. (For example, there was a different dot configuration stored for Courier 10 point, Courier 10-point italic, Courier 10-point bold, Courier 12 point, Courier 12-point italic—and on and on, for every letter in the alphabet.) Because computers had a limited amount of storage space available for these descriptions, computer users couldn't always make their type the size or style they wanted.

Adobe came up with a new way of describing letters that used a mathematical algorithm. It required much less storage and allowed computer users more choices.

Adobe's product was revolutionary. The only problem was that the company was greedy. Adobe wanted to be paid far too high a royalty whenever someone used its technology.

Microsoft approached Adobe about a new brainchild called *what you see is what you get* (WYSIWYG—pronounced "wizzy-wig.") Up to this point, computer users were unable to see how a document would look until they printed it out. With WYSIWYG, users would be able to see type fonts, italics, boldface, underlining, and other formatting right on the screen. Microsoft approached Adobe, asking if it would license the font-rendering technology for the screen so Microsoft could bundle it with Windows.

Adobe dragged its heels. It wanted to get paid whenever someone used Adobe technology. If printer companies were paying Adobe for a PostScript printer, why shouldn't Microsoft pay a per-user royalty to have the font technology for the screen? Negotiations eventually went nowhere, and Microsoft teamed up with Apple to develop a competing technology, TrueType.

This is a prime example of a competitive advantage squandered. Adobe had a product that was extremely costly to replicate, but the company made it so costly to work with Adobe that other companies decided, "We'll just replicate it."

SUMMING UP

A competitive advantage is a powerful weapon in the fight to win and maintain marketshare. It comes in four major forms:

- The virtual enterprise or increasing feedback loop
- The economic advantage
- A product that can't be replicated
- The unbeatable brand

Companies that have one of these advantages have an edge over their competition. Companies that manage to combine several of them will be even more difficult to beat.

Larry Solomon is a senior vice president at Capital International Research, part of the Capital Group of companies, which manages over $600 billion in equity assets. Larry has been a technology analyst and portfolio manager for more than 15 years and has twice been named to *Institutional Investor*'s Best of the Buyside.

Have you had any spectacular failures as an investor?

Of course. Hasn't everyone?

My most spectacular failure was probably Borland. But since Mike goes into that quite a bit elsewhere, why don't I talk about some *overarching* investment mistakes, rather than one specific stock pick.

First, let me explain how I do things. My methodology is to try to establish a framework for what the biggest growth areas and changes in technology are likely to be. Next, I figure out which companies are likely to benefit from those changes. Then I try to invest in those companies at a time when the valuation seems reasonable.

With that in mind, one of my biggest investing mistakes has been patience. When a company misexecutes, and it becomes clear that it's going to struggle, and that it's not going to become one of the main beneficiaries of a market trend, my mistake has been not taking the loss right then and there. Instead of selling the stock right away, often I've been too patient, thinking, "Well, when they just get through this period, they'll come back" and that sort of thing.

When a company is in an industry that's experiencing an explosive growth phase, initially *all* the players do well. But when the market starts to mature and, inevitably, slow down, the industry tends to consolidate around one winner. And customers usually want to buy from the winner. You have this polarity—pulling the leader even more into the lead, and pulling the other companies down. Lots of times the way that *first* manifests itself is that the number-two or number-three player misses its earnings estimates. But truth be told, that's often just the first step in a long series of misses.

Number two in my list of overarching investment mistakes: not listening to my instincts about a company's management team. That one has really gotten me into trouble on occasion.

It's important to watch the traits of successful management teams and unsuccessful management teams and find a pattern. It's important to apply that pattern.

In my experience, some of the less successful companies have *talked* ambitiously about their abilities but when you watch them in action, their ambition is sometimes much greater than their management skill. That shows up in managements that are late to meetings, or have meetings that run way over time; managements that are disorganized or out of control; those that are not totally on top of their business or who don't understand their competitors as well as their competitors understand them; managements that are unable to recruit and retain top employees; and managements that don't listen to customers—so you start to hear negative customer feedback about the company, and when it's presented to the management, they deny that those issues exist.

What was your best stock pick ever?
What did you like about it?

By far the most successful investment of my career has been Nokia. I got in early. I visited Nokia in Finland when it was only on the Finnish stock exchange. At the time, the company was a conglomerate and sold everything from televisions, to tissues, to tires—as well as having a telecommunications equipment division. I had a meeting with Nokia and was surprised by the quality, intensity, creativity, and drive of the management team.

My firm had invested very successfully in Ericcson several years prior. I decided to spend a summer in our Geneva office. One of my major reasons for going was to get to know this Finnish company that was starting to show up as a viable competitor in wireless infrastructure and cellular handsets. I visited Nokia again that summer and had a very good meeting. Then the company ended up reporting earnings that were surprisingly good. My firm began to invest.

At the time, Nokia didn't know me or even our firm particularly. The company was used to dealing with Finnish brokers, local investors, and local corporations that invested solely in other Finnish companies. Shortly thereafter, Nokia went on a roadshow to list the company's shares in London.

The first roadshow meeting was quite formal. There was assigned seating. Because I was based in the United States and didn't have a strong relationship with any brokers in London, I wasn't even assigned a seat. When the CEO sat down, I quickly sat down next to him and began peppering him with a long list of questions I'd drawn up. A broker came up to me and said, "Excuse me, that's not your seat." It was reserved for some big bank that had enough pull to be seated next to the CEO. The table everyone was seated at was shaped like an inverted C, and everyone was seated around the outside. So I got up, pulled up a chair, and put it on the *inside* of the C, right across from the CEO. I kept asking him my questions. Over the next few weeks, I went to a bunch of other meetings in other cities on the road show to ask the management team the questions I hadn't had answered yet. I was so persistent, the managers must have thought I was crazy.

But my company ended up participating in the offering in London and buying a significant chunk of shares in the aftermarket as well. In fact, we ended up buying several percent of the company. Over the years, Nokia divested the nontelecommunications portions of its business, and at the same time, the telecom business became extremely successful.

Nokia is now the number-one handset vendor in the world and one of the top three providers of wireless infrastructure in GSM, which is the largest wireless infrastructure market. The stock has probably gone up thirty- or forty-fold since our original purchase.

Do you think Nokia recognized early on that it had the potential to be such a force, even when it was a small Finnish company no one had heard of yet?

The company definitely did. I mean, I don't think at the time the management even *dreamt* of being as successful as they eventually became, but they definitely knew that success was up and to the right. They just didn't know how *far* up. But they were extremely ambitious. That was one of the things about them that was so impressive and one of the things that has continued to make them successful.

From the beginning, the management team had vision. They really understood the industry. And they applied Silicon Valley–style techniques, in Finland, to a market that was moving fairly slowly. They shortened their cycle time, they employed outsourcing *years* before competitors used outside vendors. They sourced components from merchant suppliers long before competitors did that. It gave them a cost advantage and a time-to-market advantage. At the same time, they had a tremendous understanding of the *consumer* marketplace for handsets—how the market was likely to grow in each segment. They were absolutely the most visionary and innovative managers in the industry, especially on the handset side.

Did you ever waver with Nokia, or sell any of your shares?

We decreased our holding during one period. The company encountered logistics problems in sourcing components and in having the right components for the mix of products consumers were demanding. We never sold out, but we did lighten our position. Then, when it was clear to us that Nokia was going to recover from these problems, we bought back our original position and more.

In actuality, the setback ended up being a very positive educational process for Nokia's management team because it caused them to *really* solidify their logistics process, right before the market took off. Nokia made its mistakes while the market was smaller and then when it got larger the company already had the processes in place to effectively scale up production.

What advice would you give to individual investors?

What I would suggest for individual investors is this: Find an area that you really understand—either you use the product or you're an employee in the industry. Try to find things that you think are long-lasting, big, positive trends. Then figure out who you think the biggest beneficiaries are likely to be, and invest in those companies. But before you invest in those companies, make sure that the valuation is not insane.

Follow your chosen industries really closely. Individual investors have more access to information today than I had as a *professional* investor, even five years ago. At their fingertips they can get all the SEC data, all the company data, and a slew of other information. So follow the companies. Pull up as many press releases, financial results, new product releases, and other things as you can, so that you become an expert on these companies.

My advice is to put most of your money into mutual funds; but to the extent that you want to invest in individual securities, do so with as much knowledge as possible. Invest in trends that are consistent with your view as to how the world works. There are a lot of people that probably say, "I knew that was going to be big, or I knew that company was going to be successful," but they don't follow through. For example, I used eBay as a collector of watches, and I saw the value of that company before it went public, yet I didn't invest in the company as a portfolio manager. That was a big mistake.

CHAPTER SEVEN

LOVE COMPANIES CUSTOMERS LOVE

There's a diner in New York that I go to religiously. The food's nothing special and the prices are average. But the waitress knows my "usual"—a ham-and-Swiss omelet with an English muffin instead of toast, no potatoes. Invariably, the manager walks over to say hello. She greets me by name. Neither of these things is that difficult, but the point is, the staff thinks that doing them is important. Because of their efforts, I feel more comfortable there. I leave the waitress a bigger tip, and I frequent the place loyally. It may not be Cheers, but at least somebody knows my name.

Just as restaurants with a steady stream of regulars are more likely to stay in business, companies with intense customer loyalty are more likely to last. These companies are also more likely to see their stock continue to appreciate over the years, be more immune to competitive price pressures, and be more capable of convincing customers to try a new product or service should they choose to branch out.

Loyalty is the number-one issue when it comes to ensuring repeat sales. One of the easiest ways to make customers loyal is to treat them well early on. If a company can convince someone in his or her youth that its products are the best thing since sliced bread, it has a chance at keeping that customer for life.

Before investing in any company, it's important to analyze what the typical customer thinks of the company. Vision, marketing, and management are all important company yardsticks. But to sustain growth over the long haul, companies need to develop what I call *stickiness*—something that guarantees customers will want to come back for more.

In life, everybody wants to be a hero. In business, this is often easier to accomplish than one might think, because the typical company does very little (beyond sales and other short-term incentives) to make customers love them. Companies want loyalty, but do precious little to make it happen.

What a company should really be focused on is simple—providing its customers with more than its competitors are able or willing to provide. Companies can get major bonus points and ensure devotion by doing one or all of the following:

- Providing better service
- Creating an elite product
- Delivering more value

PROVIDING BETTER SERVICE

In the early 1970s, I was living in California. The rest of my family lived in New York, and I'd fly back east about once a year to visit. I was young, and I was broke, so the most important criteria for me when choosing a flight was price.

All of that changed after I flew home by chance on American Airlines. On the way to New York, there was a problem with the in-flight movie. No matter what the flight attendants tried, it just wouldn't work. The flight attendants apologized, they turned the lights back on, they refunded our money, and we all forgot about it.

When we arrived in New York, there was an American Airlines agent waiting for us with a stack of free tickets to Radio City Music Hall, compliments of the airline. I couldn't believe it. All this over a broken movie? I was impressed.

In fact, I was so impressed that American became my airline of choice for the next 15 years. Between business and pleasure, I probably flew American at least 90 times. Dozens of sales, all because of an investment that probably cost the airline something like $5 or $10 per person.

Compare this to another experience from my youth—the Audi debacle. When I was in my late twenties, I decided to buy a new car. I had my heart set on an Audi. Audi made a good product back then, but it wasn't as popular or as expensive as it is today. Still, it was a stretch for me financially.

Once I'd scraped the money together, I called up the local dealer and asked what was in stock. He named a few colors, told me the options, and quoted me a price. I headed over, check in hand, ready to pick up the car of my dreams. When I got there, the dealer told me that the price he'd quoted was invalid. "That was the price of the car an hour ago," he said. "That's not the price now. If you want the car, it will cost you $500 more."

I was outraged. I left the dealer, went home, and called another Audi operation listed in the phone book. It was about an hour's drive. A salesperson answered the phone. Let's call him Joe. I asked what was in stock. He named three colors. I asked what the price would be. He told me. "Look," I said, "this is a long drive for me. If you tell me now that the price is a little bit higher, or that you don't have as many colors in stock as you first said, I won't be upset. You'll still make the sale. But if I drive all the way out there to find that you weren't being honest, you'll lose me."

The salesperson assured me that he was telling the truth. "That's the price. Those are the colors. Just ask for Joe, and we'll get you that car today."

I drove over there. I asked for Joe. They pointed me toward his desk. The nameplate on the desk said Joe, and there was a man sitting behind it. "Joe," I said, "I talked to you on the phone an hour ago. You quoted me this price. I'm here to buy the car."

The man shook his head. "I'm not Joe," he said. "I'm Sam. Joe hasn't been in all day. You couldn't have spoken to him on the phone. If you want a car I can get you one, but we have none in stock, so you'll have to wait. And it will cost more than what you were told."

I left the dealership. That was more than 20 years ago, and I have never since looked at an Audi, let alone bought one. There have been numerous times when my wife and I were looking for a car in that class, and an Audi would have been a great option, but we bought Volvos, or Toyotas, or anything else we could think of. We never wanted to deal with Audi again. We told everyone we knew not to deal with them, too. Audi didn't lose just one sale because of its actions, it lost many.

Why a company would intentionally choose to alienate customers is beyond me. I have no idea why Audi dealers would act like pathological liars, but it seems clear that that methodology was in the company handbook. The crazy thing is that Audi would have made the sale if the dealers had been honest with me. I would have bought a car from them, even if it cost 5 percent more than what I thought it should have. I wanted that car, and I was willing to pay what I needed to in order to get it.

But I strenuously objected to being treated so shabbily, and the fact that it happened at two different Audi dealers gave me a terrible impression of the company. If it had been only one Audi dealer, I'd have blamed it on the dealer, but because it was more than one, I associated shabby treatment with the company as a whole.

I left Audi that day and bought a Toyota. I loved it so much that I convinced seven of my friends to buy Toyotas, too. What most companies fail to realize is that if you can get customers to love you, they become an advocate for your product. People enjoy introducing their friends to the things they love.

CREATING AN ELITE PRODUCT

If your customers love you, you don't have to focus on being the cheapest. In other words, you don't have to price your products to be less profitable. A loyal customer is more interested in sticking with your brand than in saving a buck or two.

In the previous chapter I talked about one of the greatest brand builders in the world—Coca-Cola. Coke's brand has given

DOING IT RIGHT

I may be in the computer industry, but there's nothing I hate more than walking into a computer store. I find that the staff is usually either overworked, undertrained, or both. One of the main reasons Dell has rocketed to the top of the computer hardware industry is that it was able to deliver to the customer what the competition only promised: the undivided attention of a salesperson who is helpful, patient, and extremely knowledgeable.

Not only does Dell's sales staff know Dell's products backwards and forwards, the salespeople are able to intelligently steer customers toward the options that will best serve their needs. Dell is willing to build a custom machine for each customer, and consumers can do the entire transaction by phone from the comfort of their favorite easy chair, or online 24 hours a day.

Dell Computer didn't begin its life as an industry giant. The company got to the top by offering significantly better service than its competition.

the company a competitive advantage, but it has also ensured customer loyalty.

When a company builds its brand in the right way, it creates customers who love the brand so much that they're almost irrational at times. They feel good about buying the brand, and they eventually convince themselves that it tastes better. They are in love with the product—but more than that, they are in love with the *image* surrounding the product, and they want to associate themselves with that image. Not only do they want to drink Coke in public, they want to drink it in the privacy of their own homes, even if it tastes exactly the same as the generic brand. In fact, even if the generic brand is made by Coke and is only packaged differently, they are absolutely convinced that the branded product tastes better.

I know whereof I speak. When I was in graduate school, I had a group of six friends who rented a house together. None of them had much money, so they decided to share food. A month into their cohabitation, the six of them set up a rule: If anyone in the house wanted a brand name of a certain kind of food, they had to prove that they could taste the difference.

It worked this way: Whenever a roommate insisted on a certain brand name, one of the other roommates would go out and buy four different brands of the product in question. One would be the brand the person was so insistent about. The other three would be competitors or generic incarnations. Then everyone would do a taste test.

The roommate who made the purchases would lay out eight plates or glasses, two of each sample, and everyone in the house would have to rate them. No one knew which was which. If the person who'd insisted on having a certain brand-name product could correctly identify it, then the household would buy it. Otherwise, it would be no-name from then on.

Over the course of their living together, each person in the house requested a taste test several times. Each of them was absolutely positive they'd be able to correctly identify the brand they were so fanatic about. At least once a month the roommates would test out the old tastebuds, and, more often than not, I'd watch. They checked whether they could tell the difference between margarine and butter, imitation sour cream and the real thing, Coke and Pepsi, or Frito-Lay and supermarket potato chips. Of the 20 or 30 times they held these taste tests, there was only *one occasion* when a requester was actually able to pick out the favored brand correctly. I repeat: only *once!* Product loyalties may have convinced each of them that they could tell the difference, but their tastebuds said otherwise.

Now, grad school was a long time ago, and I've repeated this story many times over the years. Interestingly, almost every person I've ever told the story to is convinced that he or she could pick out favorite brands in a blind taste test.

This is especially true for soda. People are 100 percent convinced that they could pick out Coke from a tableful of competitors. At their insistence, I've run the test several times, and less than 5 percent of participants have successfully picked Coke. But the fact that so many people *believe* that they can pick out Coke shows how strong their customer loyalty lies, and it speaks volumes about Coke's brand.

When it comes to customer retention, perception is everything. The product needs to be more than the best fit for a customer, it needs to be *perceived* as the best fit. How a company markets itself has a big impact on the type of customers who will want to align themselves with the product.

E-mail is the perfect example. iVillage and Hotmail may both offer free e-mail to anyone who wants it, but the type of person who wants to identify with iVillage and the type who wants to identify with Hotmail are very different indeed. An 18-year-old male wouldn't be caught dead with an e-mail address associated with mothers and mothers-to-be.

This concept of customer image alignment is relevant to almost any company on the planet. It speaks to why a customer will reject a perfectly good cup of diner coffee for a cup of Starbucks that costs $2 more and requires a 10-minute wait. It speaks to why someone would buy a pair of Guess? jeans over a comparable pair of no-names and why someone would pay $100 more for an elite bottle of wine with the same exact quality rating as one that's readily available.

Let me tell you another story. I once had an economics professor who was a consultant for the Parker pen company. At the time, most of the pens on the market cost an average of 29 cents. Parker developed a new pen and hired my professor to help decide how to price it. At first, Parker was leaning toward charging 39 or 49 cents, but it ran some studies which showed that if the pens were priced at $2, Parker would actually sell more units than it would at the cheaper price!

The pen was nothing exceptional, but at $2 it made people *feel* exceptional. It seemed like a more elite product, and there was a market for that. Since that time, companies like Cross and Montblanc have taken advantage of this market, creating status pens that cost hundreds, even thousands of dollars. Customers have been all too happy to pay a premium for the luxury.

Customers like to feel special, and elite products allow them to feel that way. There's an interesting dichotomy in the buying habits of today's average consumers. On one hand, they want to get a good price when purchasing certain items. On the other hand, they're willing to pay a premium for products that let them treat themselves.

I recently visited a BMW dealership. I was looking at a car, and a salesperson steered me toward another part of the lot. He led me to a car called the M5 and made a point of telling me that BMW had manufactured only 2,000 of them. The price was steep, let me tell you—but the salesperson told me, "If you buy a Porsche, you'll be one of the masses. If you buy this car, you'll be one of the few."

The M5 may cost a fortune, but there are customers lining up to get one. It's amazing what people will pay in order to stand out—and it's important to factor that customer inclination into your assessment of a stock's worth.

DELIVERING MORE VALUE

A lot of companies focus on price. While price is not *un*important, according to most surveys I've read on customer behavior, price is rarely the number-one criteria customers use for buying something. It is a criteria, but it is almost never the most significant criteria.

When you're analyzing a company's products, ignore price; focus on value. *Value* might seem like a shady synonym for *price*. But the two words don't actually mean the same thing. Most consumers don't want to buy the cheapest product. They want to get the best value for the money they're willing to spend. Companies can use the following three methods to seduce these customers:

- Introducing a new product that's easier to use
- Improving existing products to expand customer benefit
- Offering a package deal

NEWER AND EASIER

The point-and-shoot camera is a prime example of a new product that is so easy to use, it brings in a previously untapped stream of customers. The new cameras had autofocus, autorewind, auto-everything. You didn't have to be a photography genius to figure them out. They were so simple to operate that they were a valuable addition to *any* household, and because of that they became a mass-market item, as opposed to a specialty one.

Similarly, the remote control led an entire generation of television viewers to go out and buy new sets. A television with a remote made watching so much more enjoyable that scores of consumers decided it was worth replacing their old sets just so they could utilize the new technology.

EXPANDING CUSTOMER BENEFIT

Yahoo! started off with a bang. It was the most compelling portal on the Web. Soon, though, other companies began to replicate Yahoo!'s services, and customers had absolutely nothing to lose by switching to someone else.

In order to transform its visitors into loyal customers, Yahoo! created My Yahoo!, a new service that allowed its users to customize Yahoo! to suit their individual tastes and interests. It took awhile to jump through all the hoops, and optimizing My Yahoo! required frequent updates. But customers who went to the trouble could get a Yahoo! home page with their favorite news filtered for them, real-time stock quotes on their favorite investments, and more.

Not only was this a benefit to the customer, it provided Yahoo! with some much-needed stickiness. The customization process took a long time, and customers who'd gone through it were much less likely to jump ship. If they switched to another portal, they'd have to start from scratch.

Another example of expanded customer benefit comes from the airline industry. Carriers were having trouble convincing travelers to choose one airline consistently, so they introduced frequent-flyer clubs. Repeat customers were offered free travel, upgrades, preferred seating, and other perks for sticking with one airline, as opposed to shopping around. Rewarding customer loyalty with expanded benefits revolutionized the airline industry. Visa took things one step further by introducing a credit card that allowed customers to rack up free air miles. The result was customer allegiance and a chunk of American Express's market share.

THE PACKAGE DEAL

A price war, if a company is intent on fighting one, can be waged without a true cost advantage by bundling a product with some extras. Let's face it, there's nothing quite like the light in a customer's eyes when he or she is offered "something for nothing." An astute company can use this universal customer truth to its advantage by providing a package that appears valuable to the customer, but costs only marginally more to produce than the original product.

The most obvious example is the cosmetics gift set offered to customers who spend a minimum amount at the counter. The gift sets are primarily made up of sample-size moisturizers and makeup overstock, but women flock to department store makeup departments to cash in on the freebies. In order to do so, they usually must buy more than they had originally planned, as the minimum amount is cleverly set to be just slightly more than the price of any individual product. Nevertheless, both customer and business benefit.

The fast-food market has turned package deals into an art form. Let's say a guy goes into McDonald's, craving a Big Mac. At the register, he's told that for 50 cents more he can add fries and a soda. Even if he wasn't planning on buying them, at *that* price he'll usually spring for the Value Meal.

The Suite Spot

Microsoft is not McDonald's, but its employees may have picked up a thing or two from too many fast-food runs. The Microsoft suite concept is the Value Meal of software.

Before the introduction of product suites, a customer had to separately purchase word-processing, spreadsheet, graphics, and database programs. Each one had a fairly substantial cost, and there was no monetary incentive to buy them all.

Microsoft decided to shake things up by bundling its Word word processor, its Excel spreadsheet, and its PowerPoint graphics program into what it called a *suite*. Conceptually, Microsoft was saying that for about 50 percent more than you'd pay for one application, you could get three.

Three for the price of one and a half! This brought the price per application down by 50 percent. When Microsoft first introduced the suite concept, many analysts thought the company was crazy. They were convinced that the suite packaging would eat away at Microsoft's revenue.

I saw things differently. When I looked at what was in the suite, I realized that there wasn't much overlap between the users of each of the products. In other words, each product's penetration into the others' camps was fairly low. I decided that if Microsoft could sell the suite to its customers, revenues would actually rise, because people would be convinced to pay for more than they'd usually buy.

Think of the suite as an all-in-one stereo or an automobile option package. A customer looking to buy a CD player may be swayed to buy a stacked system that costs marginally more, but includes a tape deck and amplifier. A car buyer may arrive at the dealership wanting to buy a baseline model with air conditioning. But he or she may be convinced to pay marginally more for an option package that includes air conditioning, mudguards, and wheel covers—extras that bring the bill up significantly but cost the dealer next to nothing. Similarly, the cost to Microsoft of creating a suite was extremely low. The biggest expense was the packaging, which the company kept to a minimum.

I liked the suite strategy because I saw that it would allow Microsoft to collect more *total dollars* per customer. If Microsoft could get the Big Mac fan to pay a little more for the fries and soda, so to speak, it would be a win-win situation. The average customer would buy 3 applications instead of the previous average of 1.1 applications (see Figure 7.1).

Customers like freebies, but they aren't stupid. When creating a suite, companies need to make sure that the individual products within it are attractive in their own right, and the products need to have perceived value in order to be attractive. Otherwise, customers think they're buying something cheap, rather than something valuable.

Suites also need to make a sensible package. A value meal that includes a Big Mac, hot cakes, and six McNuggets isn't as attractive a package as one with an Egg McMuffin, hash browns, and coffee.

FIGURE 7.1   ANALYSIS OF MICROSOFT'S SUITE STRATEGY.

General Analysis						
WORD	EXCEL	POWER-POINT	TOTAL PRICE	SUITE PRICE	DISCOUNT	CONCLUSION
$230	$230	$225	$685	$375	45%	Bad

Mike's Analysis					
AVERAGE PURCHASE	PRICE	TOTAL SPENT	SUITE PRICE	ADDITIONAL REVENUE	CONCLUSION
1.1 products	$230	$253	$375	48%	Good

It's vital for a package deal's success that the products within it complement each other.

Smoking Out the Competition

The best thing about the package deal is that it helps to prevent trespassing. Before introducing suites, Microsoft competed with WordPerfect, Software Publishing, Lotus, Borland, and a slew of other companies on a single-application basis. Each program had to fend for itself. Word competed with WordPerfect. Excel had to contend with Lotus 1-2-3. PowerPoint was up against Harvard Graphics.

Once suites entered the picture, the rules changed entirely. Now it was the team that mattered most, not the individual players. Gone was the need to be the best in each category. A strong *combination* of products was the key to victory. Microsoft began the suite race with a huge advantage—the company was the only contender with compelling products in all three product categories.

Microsoft's head start forced competitors to try to join forces. Software Publishing trolled the waters for partners. Novell bought WordPerfect and Quattro Pro. Lotus acquired Ami Pro.

The pressure to integrate took its toll. Novell's market share plummeted while the company tried to fuse the old and the new.

Novell's profitability eventually became so endangered that it had to sell WordPerfect, for a song, to Corel. Lotus, which had acquired Ami Pro in order to create a suite, ran into problems integrating Freelance, its presentation product, and fell very far behind. Software Publishing, creator of Harvard Graphics, never came to an agreement with anybody and was eliminated from the competition altogether. In short, all the competitors encountered problems trying to unite, integrate, or create a set of applications that could compete with Microsoft, whose products were already among the best of the breed in every category.

After the smoke had cleared, only two major competitors remained: Lotus and Corel. Lotus sold itself to IBM. Corel was hanging on by its fingernails.

PRICING FOR THE MASSES

One of the things that made Microsoft such a superpower was Bill Gates's philosophy of pricing for the masses. Gates started out with a simple motto, "A computer on every desktop," and he priced software in a way that would help make that dream a reality. In fact, if it hadn't become a reality, the pricing probably would have driven his company bankrupt. In order for Microsoft's pricing to work, its products had to reach mass-market distribution.

Pricing software low enough that the masses could afford to buy it was somewhat revolutionary, but it made perfect sense to Gates. If the company sold its software to every single hardware vendor and got them all to bundle it with their machines, the unit cost to Microsoft on each piece of software would be essentially nothing. Plus, Microsoft would achieve massive acceptance at almost zero cost of goods. Thousands of hardware vendors could also load tons of software onto their machines for less money, making their computers more valuable to the customer.

There's a very famous memo that was sent to John Sculley by a young Bill Gates. In the memo, Gates urged Sculley (the CEO of Apple) to license the Mac operating system and make it available to hardware vendors other than Apple. If you do this, Gates promised, Apple will become the dominant vendor in operating systems. Sculley ignored Gates's advice. After all, Apple could make lots of profits on each unit if it didn't open it up. If Apple licensed the Mac OS, there would be competition, and maybe Apple wouldn't make as much money.

Here lies a major difference in philosophy. Whereas Apple felt it was better to make more money on each of hundreds of thousands of units, Microsoft felt that it would eventually sell 100 million units and make plenty of money.

In a way, Gates was heir to the throne of the great monopolists like Henry Ford. In 1908, Ford changed the future of the automobile industry, not only by inventing the Model T but by figuring out a way to produce it so inexpensively that it would be affordable to the masses. Ford's assembly line process changed the entire economics of automobile production and sales.

Bill Gates could well be called the Henry Ford of his generation. Conceptually, Microsoft has thought things through for software in precisely the same way that Ford did for automobiles. The car manufacturers before Ford handcrafted each car and made it to the specifications of a single customer. Similarly, before Microsoft, a lot of the software manufacturers created a custom piece of software for a single type of hardware. Software development costs per unit were astronomical because all software was proprietary.

PUTTING IT TOGETHER

Identifying companies that customers love is not an exact science. But at the core, all investors are consumers. Before investing in a stock, ask yourself what the company does to attract and retain its customers. If you can, buy the product. Test the customer experience first-hand.

When I first started analyzing Gateway and Compaq, I was also in the market for a computer. I bought a Gateway, and at about the same time, my daughter Danielle bought a Compaq. The contrast was startling. When we went shopping for the Compaq, it was clear that no one in any of the retail outlets knew what they were talking about. They hadn't been properly trained about the product line. Compaq's prices, compared to similar Gateway models, were excessive. Once Danielle got the Compaq up to school, things got even worse. Technical support was awful. On two different occasions, phone support people gave her incorrect information that actually crashed her machine. One of these episodes nearly wiped her hard disk.

You don't need to buy a product to test it, but it's a good idea to sample the buying experience. Call the company's order hotline or check out its Web site. Go to a store that carries the line. See what the buying experience is like as a customer. How long do you have to wait? Do the sales advisors know the product line inside and out? Are your questions answered intelligently? Is everything in stock?

Customers tend to gravitate toward award-winning products. They're status items, elite. Check out the company's Web site. Look at the investor relations page for any customer service or related awards. Don't limit your Web tour to your potential investment's site. See how its competitors tout themselves, and check if they've won acclaim. Look in industry magazines and analyze product and customer satisfaction ratings. Use your favorite search engine (www.ask.com, www.yahoo.com, www.excite.com, and www.google.com are my top picks) for articles. If the company produces a consumer item, browse through *Consumer Reports* magazine. If it makes tech products, check out ZDNet, Forrester Research, CNET, *Wired* magazine, or *HotWired*. Compare your pick to its competitors, and see how it matches up in value and characteristics.

Most important, ask yourself if you would love this company. Would you stay true? A good customer relationship is like a good romance—hard to find and even harder to maintain.

SUMMING UP

To acquire customers and encourage commitment, businesses need to do at least one of the following things:

- Provide better service.
- Offer an elite product.

- Deliver more value:

  Introduce a new product that's easier to use.

  Improve an old product to expand customer benefit.

  Offer a package deal.

Fred Kobrick was an equity portfolio manager at State Street until 1997, when he left to start his own firm. Since that time, the Kobrick Capital Fund has been selected for *USA Today*'s 25 All-Star Funds each year. For two years out of three, it was Fund of the Year. *Money* magazine called the Kobrick Capital Fund one of the six best funds of the decade, and *USA Today* called it "one of the best five funds for the *entire* bull market." In 1999, the Kobrick Capital Fund returned 89.1 percent; during the 1990s as a whole, the funds Kobrick managed have had returns of more than 500 percent. He appears regularly as a stockpicker in Peter Lynch's *Worth* magazine roundtable.

What was the most you ever made on a single stock?

The best stock I ever owned was Cisco. I thought it would double in a year after the IPO, but that it would then see competition catching up. The stock doubled from 11 cents to 22 cents, but Cisco actually *lengthened* its lead over the competition. I could see how well it was managed, and how and why the company's customers loved it, and its great culture and management, so I added to the position and did a 17-bagger after the double!

What was your worst investment in recent memory?

Sunglass Hut. It was a great growth story for some time, but blew up and went down 60 percent. The company bit off far more than it could chew and failed to execute. It was also far too optimistic. My mistake was that after enjoying much success with the company, and knowing top management was good, I didn't press to see if it had the middle management to execute what it was trying to do. The big lesson I learned was that the sexier the story, the harder—not easier—it is to execute, and that companies must have a great management team and execution culture to continue to succeed.

What is your most important criteria when looking at investing in a company?

There are thousands of buy recommendations from Wall Street, television, magazines, your best friends, and at cocktail parties every year. They are mainly based on a good earnings story and good valuations. Most do not work out because they don't have a good enough management team to execute the plan and win the game. To me management is 80 percent of the story. I have developed the management interview and the analysis of management's ability to execute as both an art and a science. It is the heart of what I do best.

If you had five minutes in which to impart your wisdom to the individual investor, what advice would you give?
Most individual investors buy some of the greatest companies—Microsoft, Home Depot, Sun Microsystems, Dell Computer—from their childhood to older age, and don't differentiate those companies or great mutual funds from ordinary companies and ordinary mutual funds. They don't understand what a great manager or great company is. They buy and sell on momentum. Because of that, they never get the long ride. My best advice is to do lots of investigating before and during the holding period and do that differentiating, looking most of all for the long ride.

CHAPTER EIGHT

LOOK FOR LONG-TERM THINKERS

Have you ever heard the fable of the scorpion and the frog? If so, forgive me while I butcher it. If not, here's an approximation:

Once upon a time, there was a scorpion who needed to get across a river. The river was deep, and the scorpion couldn't swim. He knew that if he tried to cross it on his own, he'd drown. Just as the scorpion was beginning to get discouraged, he saw a frog sitting on the bank. "Frog," he said, "let me ride on your back while you swim across the river. For this I will be grateful."

The frog was suspicious of the scorpion. "If I let you ride on my back, who says you won't bite me?" he replied.

The scorpion laughed and assured him that biting was out of the question. "How could I bite you?" the scorpion said. "Then you'd be poisoned and both of us would drown."

The frog thought things over and decided that what the scorpion said made sense. So he knelt down, let the scorpion climb aboard, and started heading across the river. About a mile from shore, the scorpion bit. As the frog felt the poison shoot through his body, with about a minute left to live, the frog croaked, "Why did you bite me? You can't swim! Now both of us will die. Why did you do it?"

The scorpion shrugged. "I couldn't help it," he said, "It's just my nature."

Now I love a good story, but I'm not telling this one just to pass the time. As strange as it may seem, the fable of the scorpion and the frog wonderfully illustrates the concept of long-term thinking. Most high-tech companies—as good as they seem on paper, as good as they sound in the news—will ultimately fail. Do you know why? Because they think like the scorpion.

You probably know some people who revel in short-term gratification—people who perpetually max out their credit cards, buy things they can't afford, live beyond their means, and don't see any problem with that. In fact, you may have even envied these people. From afar, they seem to be living it up. The problem is, it's all downhill from here. Over the years the scorpion gets further and further behind until it's a struggle just to keep afloat.

Unfortunately for the U.S. economy, much of the business world is comprised of short-term thinkers. Why? Because most executives are rewarded for short-term performance—their bonuses are dependent on how they do *this year*. Plus, they have stock options, and if they can manage to do something dramatic and drive the stock up over the short term, they can cash it in and eke out a nice little nest egg. Considering the speed with which many of these high-tech companies fold, the company might not even be around for the long term, so immediate performance is very important.

PRIME EXAMPLES OF SHORT-TERM THINKING

High-tech companies don't have the patent on short-term thinking. Many other industries have sunk because the people in charge focused only on the present. The automobile industry is a prime example.

There was a saying when I was growing up: "As General Motors goes, so goes the nation." Seeing GM now, this may be hard to believe, but there was a time when the company was so integral to the U.S. economy in terms of the number of people it employed, the profits it generated, and its volume of exports, that its performance was a critical factor in how the country was doing as a whole.

In its heyday, GM had something like a 50 percent market share of the worldwide automobile business. It was so dominant that no one could even *imagine* that any other company had even a chance of overtaking GM—especially a foreign company, because the number-two car manufacturer was Ford.

What happened? Scorpion thinking, my friend. GM got into some very bad habits. It was so consumed with maximizing each year's profits that it lost all sense of the larger mission.

For example, at a certain juncture GM decided that it could produce higher profits if all GM cars had the same engine. The company told one of its subsidiaries to start making engines for almost all of the vehicles in its product line. Then GM decided to take things a step further. Why not put the same body on every one of its models? If all of GM's cars looked the same, things would get even cheaper.

While GM was busy adjusting the *externals* in order to shave off a few bucks here and there, Japanese and European carmakers were investing heavily in the *internals* of their vehicles. They focused on quality control and customer support. They improved their warranties, bundled more features into their cars, and pioneered safety measures like seat belts and airbags.

Unlike most American carmakers, which were focused on quarterly profits, the Japanese manufacturers were focused on long-term market domination. Aware of the extremely poor reputation they'd garnered early on as carmakers, the Japanese companies decided to concentrate on vehicle dependability.

Unlike their American counterparts, the Japanese were willing to be very patient in launching their brands and gaining market share. To help the process along, companies like Honda began to offer their initial models at incredible values. Buyers in the market for a car found it difficult to ignore Honda vehicles. Hondas offered much more than other cars in the same price range.

Similarly, when Toyota launched the Lexus, it gave a phenomenal amount of bang for the buck. When customers compared the Lexus to the other offerings in its class—Mercedes and BMW—there was no comparison. First-class features combined with a bargain price tag created a huge market for the Lexus brand right from the get-go. Then, because the car's quality was so good, consumers came back again and again, even when Toyota raised Lexus prices.

What foreign carmakers understood, and companies like GM failed to realize, was that cheap was not enough. Selling customers something cheap at a cheap price didn't hold a candle to selling them something of quality at a fair price. While Japanese carmakers focused on performance, GM concerned itself with adjusting cosmetics to improve each year's bottom line.

GM hit the mark. Profits soared the year of the one-size-fits-all engine and communal car body. But at what cost? The Cadillac owner now had a car with the same body and the same engine as a Pontiac. This was not the best way to enhance the image of the Cadillac as a luxury vehicle.

In just a few years, GM managed to almost completely erode the reputation of its brands. By the time GM finally awakened to the problem, its market share had disintegrated. Worse yet, young people getting ready to buy their first cars didn't share the old view of GM products.

Profits come and go, but perception is hard to change. GM had created a perception that was almost impossible to turn around. To some extent, it's still trying. Over the past few years, GM has invested heavily in image and, to some extent, quality. But GM has never been able to truly recapture the aura it once had.

Going Long

Take GM's mistakes to heart. Beware of scorpion management. It will poison even the most promising investments.

When you're shopping for stocks for your portfolio, you need to look for companies that are interested in more than just short-term gratification. Look for companies that have their eyes trained on the opposite bank, companies that are intent on getting all the way across the river, even if it means a less impressive quarter.

Long-term thinking is paramount to success. In order for a company to have many years of high-level growth and performance, its management team has to resist the urge to grab all it can up front. That said, it's time for a pop quiz:

You are Bill Gates. What would you do in each of the following situations?

- You're a kid. Your mom offers you a choice: She will give you an allowance of $30 a week to buy all the video games and candy your little heart desires, or you can choose to receive zippo until the end of the year, when you'll get a lump sum of $5,000. Which do you take?

- You own a company, and several important customers are upset about one of your products. You can appease them and be sure you'll retain their accounts (each of which generates at least $10 million a year in business for you), but to do so you'll have to spend a hefty $10,000 on each customer. Or, you can decide to save the money, reinvest it in your business, and take your chances that they'll buy from you again. Which do you do?

- Your company has a new product, and you can't decide how much to charge for it. Some of your employees want to charge $100 a unit; others want to charge $10,000. There's really no competing product at this point in time, and the product costs you very little to produce. If you charge $10,000 for the product, you'll probably get about 1,000 customers in the first year (about $10 million in revenue), and sales will grow by 10 percent a year for the next 10 years (to $27 million). On the other hand, if you charge $100 for the product, at least 10,000 customers will buy the product in the first year ($1 million in revenue), and sales will triple every year. Which do you do?

Remember, I asked what *Bill Gates* would do. But the truth is, I'm absolutely certain what his choice would be in each and every case.

Gates would take $5,000 at the end of the year for his allowance, he'd invest the $10,000 per account to keep those customers happy, and he'd charge $100 per unit rather than $10,000.

Why am I so sure? Look at his record: Gates is a long-term thinker to his core. Any long-term thinker can see that the lasting benefits of each of these decisions will far exceed the short-term gains one would enjoy by playing the other side.

PRIME EXAMPLES OF LONG-TERM THINKING

Anyone reading this book will be familiar by now with my penchant for Microsoft and Dell. I love these companies for many reasons, but one of the main reasons is long-term thinking.

MICROSOFT

I'm the first to admit it: Windows 1.0 was a dud, and so was 2.0. By the time version 3.0 came out, Windows as a whole was widely viewed as a failure. However, Windows 3.0 was a turning point— not just for Microsoft, but for the computer industry as a whole. For the first time, there was significant buzz about a PC operating system. Even before its release, people were talking: This was the version that was finally going to *work!*

With the buzz over Windows 3.0 in mind, a lot of developers started putting their products on Windows. At the same time, Microsoft itself placed Word, Excel, and anything else it had on the platform. By the time Windows 3.0 was officially released, it was clear that over time it would become the dominant product.

Windows 3.0 was the beginning of Microsoft's real run at success. It was also the beginning of a strain of gossip that has haunted Microsoft for years—that the company can't get it together until version 3. Part of this, of course, implies that Microsoft can't manage to do things right the first time. But I'd argue that it also points to something equally true: Microsoft doesn't give up until it *does* get things right.

Now, I've already admitted that Windows 1.0 and 2.0 were pretty bad products. But what's interesting is *what* was bad about them. Windows itself needed more work, but its main problem was that the computers of the day didn't have enough power to run a Windows-type program well.

This second liability is important to understand, because it perfectly illustrates Gate's penchant for long-term thinking. Sure, Microsoft released a product that was not quite optimal—but what Gates understood was the fact that it would *soon be* optimal.

It's a well-known fact that the power of computer processors grows extremely rapidly. In fact, it doubles every 18 months. The amount of disk drive and memory in the average new computer also doubles. Gates took these facts into account and recognized that in a few years, computers would have four times the power they did at the time of Windows 1.0's release—more than enough to eventually run the program.

The truth is, Microsoft was well aware that Windows wasn't ready when it put Windows 1.0 and 2.0 on the market. It put two flawed versions out in order to gain experience with the product and to get some people using it. Gates knew that by the time computers were ready for Windows to be a *mass-market* product, the program and the company would be ready, because Microsoft would have invested in Windows for enough years to *make* it ready.

Ten years later, Microsoft has essentially repeated this same long-term strategy with NT Server. It has invested heavily for a number of years, gone through several generations of the product, and finally gotten it right. What's important to understand is that the *finally* was in the original game plan, as were the shaky interim years.

Microsoft adopted a mass-market strategy with NT Server, much like the one it had adopted with Windows. The company started with a product that was consistently less costly than the leading competitor (in this case, Unix). Then it courted the buzz and tried to coax as many equipment manufacturers as possible onto the platform, so there would be enough applications to woo customers. Microsoft worked the kinks out in full view of the public with a few early versions, knowing that by getting into servers early enough, it would have a chance to eventually dominate the marketplace. Most important, Microsoft acted like it was the number-one contender in the market long before it actually was. That level of commitment and confidence eventually brought it there.

DELL

Dell Computer didn't start off with a bang—it started off with Michael Dell building machines in his dorm room between classes. It grew slowly to include a real staff, and like a giant snowball rolling down a hill, it picked up momentum along the way. Dell's growth was no accident. It was the direct result of a CEO who could envision the future and had the patience to work toward it.

Michael Dell realized that the future of hardware was the direct-sales model (see Chapter 6). What's interesting about the direct-sales model, in terms of long-term thinking, is that it requires patience. Although going direct offers a competitive advantage *eventually*, it takes time.

A company can develop much more quickly by going through retail channels, because it doesn't need to have as many people and as much infrastructure in place. It can gear up more rapidly because retailers provide the salespeople, the shelf space, and the support.

When you're a direct seller, someone on your payroll has to sell every single machine. Someone on your payroll has to support each and every customer with a problem. If you, like Dell, offer custom machines as an option, someone on your payroll has to assemble those custom machines for every single customer who orders one, making manufacturing much more complicated.

All of these things add up to one reality: It takes much longer to build a direct-model company than it does to sell products through the retail channel. A new company can't hire enough people to sell, support, and build a million machines the first year it's in business, so business grows gradually.

Michael Dell approached individual products in the same way he approached his business as a whole—with a long-term attitude. With each product Dell introduced after the desktop PC, the management didn't expect immediate gratification. Whether the product was a notebook computer, a server, or storage, Dell took a similar tack: Hire an unbelievable team, give employees whatever timeline they need to create excellence, encourage lengthy development, and invest heavily in the product—even if it takes years to see any significant revenue.

With PC servers, Dell entered the race with less than 1 percent market share. Michael Dell was well aware of the fight ahead, but he was confident that with perseverance, Dell could eventually surpass industry giants like Compaq, Hewlett-Packard, and IBM. Dell started modestly. It entered the server arena on the low end. It hired an unbelievable team of superstars who gradually worked their way up through the product line. Along the way, Dell formed partnerships with Intel and Microsoft to help strengthen its position. Seven years later, Dell had propelled itself into the number-two place with servers and was quickly closing the gap between itself and Compaq, the leading player.

Because Dell recognizes the power of long-term thinking, I have every confidence in its ability to keep coming out on top, regardless of whatever new market it chooses to conquer. For the past year, Dell's profit growth has been less than stellar, and many investors have concluded that the party's over. I beg to differ. Anyone who looks to the reasons behind the recent shortfall in profits will notice a pattern—*seeding*.

Here's just one example: Dell's profits took a hit while it was pouring money into the Web. The result of the monetary outpouring was a system that is capable of outpacing all but a precious few customer support representatives. It includes an *intelligent support system* along the lines of the search engine Ask Jeeves—customers can type in a question, and the system will send back a useful response.

Miraculously, the thing actually works. Plus, there's no telephone hold time, no cost, and no workday—the system is up 24 hours a day, 7 days a week. Is it worth the short-term profit reduction? Dell thinks so. The company realized that over the long-term, transferring sales and support online would save it a bundle. Already Dell is doing billions of dollars a year in online sales.

AMAZON

If there's any company that is putting long-term thinking to the test, it's Amazon. Amazon has taken the concept of being unprofitable to a new level. Public for four years now, Amazon has done the unbelievable, shown a tremendous *increase* in losses quarter after quarter, with few apologies. Lots of people on Wall Street doubt that the company will ever turn a profit.

My own belief is that Amazon may have already turned the corner on profitability with its book business. But because it has immediately reinvested any book profits into other areas, things still look lousy on paper. Jeff Bezos, Amazon's CEO, believes that in order to win as a customer brand, an online bookstore has to have a span of products beyond books. He believes that the Web has yet to be won, and that time is short. In order to guarantee longevity as a dot-com company, Bezos believes that a company has to make an immediate land grab. Any company that hopes to win out on the Web needs to make the grab now, and quickly—as quickly as its shareholders will allow without crashing the stock completely.

There's no question that Bezos is a long-term thinker. The question is whether he is right. Time will tell. I personally think that Bezos's thinking has Amazon poised to be the Wal-Mart of the web. However, at this writing, Wall Street clearly disagrees with me.

SUMMING UP

- Long-term thinking is paramount to success.
- In order to have high-level growth for a number of years, companies need to resist the urge to grab all they can up front.
- Look for management teams that are focused on *lasting* results.
- To stay for the duration, companies need to invest heavily in the future, even if it means damaging near-term profits.

Roger McNamee is cofounder of Integral Capital Partners and Silver Lake Partners. He was recently dubbed "a scary-smart tech investor" by *Fortune* and one of the "Top 25 Power Brokers in Silicon Valley" by *BusinessWeek.*

What big investment mistakes have you made, and what did they teach you?

Great question. I had a terrible summer of 1990. It was a horrible period for technology investors—the Iraqi invasion of Kuwait caused a sell-off that crushed the tech sector—but I made it much worse by my own actions (or inactions).

At the time, I was managing the T. Rowe Price Science & Technology Fund and comanaging the T. Rowe Price New Horizons Fund. We owned huge positions in three stocks—Oracle, Ultimate Corporation, and Apollo Computer—which had done well, but where we grossly overstayed our welcome. I made the same mistake in all three cases—I relied too much on assurances from management that all was well.

There was evidence of business problems at all three companies. In the case of Oracle and Ultimate (an enterprise software company focused on medium-sized businesses), these related to revenue recognition. In Apollo's case, the company was getting outmarketed by Sun.

The founders of Oracle and Ultimate were charismatic, but tended to exaggerate. In each case the senior management team was motivated by arbitrary revenue growth targets—100 percent per year—and had no qualms about stretching the rules to make numbers. I convinced myself that nothing had really changed—the companies had always behaved that way—and that I couldn't afford not to own the stocks. I ignored my better instincts, which were telling me that Oracle and Ultimate had rotten business practices which should have caused me to sell the stocks.

Lesson learned: Bad business practices will eventually lead to big trouble. If you don't like what the team is doing, don't own the stock. Even if it's going up.

Apollo's management wasn't messing around with the accounting rules. They just didn't understand their end market. I convinced myself that the stock was cheap relative to Sun. If Apollo had made the numbers, that would have been true. The problem was that Apollo couldn't sell enough computers to make the numbers.

Lesson learned: Purchasers of information technology want to buy from the market leader. The market leader always looks expensive, relative to its competitors—but it will still make you more money. If the category is a relatively large one—as Sun's market turned out to be—it will make you a lot more money.

Final words of wisdom?

Understand your risk tolerance before you invest. If you are going to be greedy, be long-term greedy, not short-term greedy. Never be in a hurry. Invest only in businesses you understand.

CHAPTER NINE

ALWAYS LOOK FORWARD, NOT BACKWARD

T here is no such thing as a safe stock. There are *unsafe* stocks. There are *safer* stocks. But there is no such thing as a *safe* stock.

That said, it may surprise you to learn that the stocks that *appear* the safest—those that sport a pedigree from the most well-entrenched, well-established companies out there—are often the dogs of the Dow. Why? Because the stock market is prejudiced against companies that aren't part of the in crowd. The *in crowd* consists of old-timers with proven reputations and newcomers that have been anointed as sure winners.

The average investor is more comfortable investing in a company that's been around since he or she was sitting on grandpa's knee, or else slapping down his or her savings for a newly minted sensation. Average investors invest in what everybody else is talking about. They don't have the time or the inclination to study reality or to do the work necessary to dig for an underappreciated opportunity. Unfortunately, sticking to these types of stocks virtually guarantees that these investors will never attain a 25 percent return on their portfolios.

BETTING ON THE OLD-TIMERS

The world keeps changing, but many people refuse to change with it. They're modern-day Rip van Winkles: They pick a few old-timers—companies that they can't imagine could ever go under—and then fall asleep in their coffee. Twenty years later, they wake up from their slumber, yawn a big yawn, and check out their portfolios. At this point, two facts become blindingly clear: (1) Most of these companies still exist, and (2) they haven't done very much for their stockholders' money.

May I introduce the Nifty 50? These darlings of the late 1960s and early 1970s were dubbed stocks so safe that you could buy them for your pregnant grandmother and still sleep at night. The 50 companies were considered "one-decision stocks"—in other words, buy them and forget about them. Those investors patient enough to sit on their holdings for the long term were promised double-digit profit growth, year after year.

Sounds good, no? The only problem was that these supersafe bets proved to be anything but. If you had bought Polaroid in 1973 and held on tight, you'd be sitting on a loss today. Avon would have pulled in a whopping $3 per share over the long haul. Xerox, one of the better performers, is up about $16 a share, but keep in mind that when you divide that gain over the years that have passed, it comes out to an annualized return of less than 1 percent. Not all of the stocks were absolutely awful (for example, Coca-Cola yielded a 17 percent compound annual return), but overall, the 50 proved to be not so nifty. Nine of the companies either no longer exist or no longer trade publicly. The total return from the 50 from December 1972 to May 1995 was only 10.08 percent per year, which was less than the return from the S&P 500.

BETTING ON THE NEW WUNDERKIND

If they're not focused on the established and well-entrenched companies, the bulk of investors are hot on the latest dot-com or another flavor of the month. You know what I'm talking about. This is the kind of company you read about in the headlines and

COMPOUND ANNUAL RETURN

Also sometimes called the *compound annual growth rate* (CAGR), compound annual return is the interest rate required for an initial investment to reach a certain critical mass in a specified time period, as a result of both interest on the initial amount and interest on the interest that accumulates.

For example, suppose someone told you that an investment would double your money in six years. For $100 to become $200 in six years, you'd need an annual interest rate, or CAGR, of about 12.25 percent (see Figure 9.1). For the money to double in three years, the CAGR would have to be about 26 percent:

- At 26 percent return, $100 would grow to $126 in one year.

- In the second year, the interest would be applied to $126. 26 percent of $126 is $32.76. Adding the $32.76 in interest to the $126 principal means you would have $158.76 at the end of the second year.

- In the third year, the 26 percent interest would be applied to your $158.76, which brings the total up to slightly over $200.

The key thing to realize is that compounding means earning interest on interest. If you had earned 26 percent each year on only the original $100, then you would have three years of $26 returns and wind up with a total of $178 (the original $100 plus 3 times the $26).

hear discussed on television. The CEO's face appears everywhere you turn, and everybody seems to be talking about him or her.

This kind of sensation can be tempting. After all, would a company anointed by the media and analysts everywhere be risky? You bet. It can be very risky. If you can get in on the IPO, great. If not, you're taking a big risk. Once a company is on the general radar, especially at such magnitude, it's often trading at hundreds of times beyond next year's consensus revenue. When a stock is val-

FIGURE 9.1   DOUBLING A $100 INVESTMENT.

YEAR	BEGIN YEAR AMOUNT	INTEREST RATE	INTEREST	END YEAR AMOUNT
1	$100.00	12.25%	$12.25	$112.25
2	112.25	12.25	13.75	125.99
3	125.99	12.25	15.43	141.42
4	141.42	12.25	17.32	158.74
5	158.74	12.25	19.44	178.18
6	178.18	12.25	21.82	200.00
1	100.00	26.00	26.00	126.00
2	126.00	26.00	32.76	158.76
3	158.76	26.00	41.28	200.04

ued at 250 times next year's revenue estimate, even if it's growing at 100 percent annually, it will be extremely difficult for it to do well over the next few years, despite the hype.

Consider VA Linux, a company that I recently helped take public. Some of my friends, hearing that my firm would be leading the IPO, asked me about VA Linux a few days before it was to officially hit the market.

My firm had announced that the IPO price would be $30 per share. Because the company was a huge player in the Linux space, I expected the price to run well beyond that within the first few hours of trading. I didn't know by how much, but I told my friends that if VA Linux traded comparably to Cobalt (a Linux hardware company) or Red Hat (a Linux software and services company), it would go up quite a bit. I thought it could easily reach $125 by the time the market closed that day. I told my friends that if they could get in on the IPO through their broker, to consider it, but that they should under no circumstances pay more than $100 a share on the open market.

At the crack of dawn on the day of the IPO, my friends spoke to their broker. They asked him what he thought the stock would open at. He told them $30, the IPO price. Based on his assessment, they put in a market order for 100 shares.

VA Linux turned out to be the best-ever performing IPO on its first day of trading, closing up more than 700 percent above the IPO price. The stock opened at $300 per share, traded as high as $320, and eventually closed at about $250 per share. But despite the run-up, many individual investors lost their shirts that day. All market orders were executed at $300 per share or more. Many of the people who bought into VA Linux between $300 and $320, and didn't sell for a quick loss, lost 50 percent or more on their money.

Unfortunately, my friends were in that group. Their stock was bought at $300, and as it started to plummet, they were torn as to what to do. They ended up selling half of their shares within the first three trading days, at about $200 each, but the damage was already done.

My friends broke the cardinal rule of investing in a high-tech IPO: *Never, never, never put in a market order on a hot commodity.* What did they do wrong? First of all, they trusted their broker. Anyone who's ever followed a high-tech IPO knows that these stocks *never* open at the IPO price, and the broker certainly should have known that. His belief that the stock would open at $30, the IPO price, was just plain ridiculous. Adding insult to injury, my friends *bought high,* and they then had few options, other than holding onto their remaining stock and waiting for it to rebound or else *selling low.*

If they decide to wait, they may have to wait awhile. At this writing, VA Linux has just reported two of the best quarters in the history of any public company—its revenue was up 537 percent in its first public quarter and more than 700 percent in its second. However, despite the numbers, VA Linux's stock currently sits at $33 per share, less than 14 times next year's consensus revenue (as compared to about 100 times at the close of the first day of trading). Despite extremely good news, VA Linux has traded down considerably (see Figure 9.2).

Now don't get me wrong—over the next few years I expect this to be a great stock or I wouldn't have taken the company public,

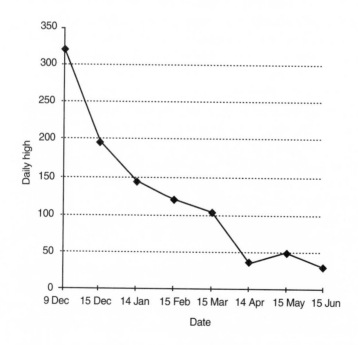

FIGURE 9.2 **VA LINUX STOCK CHART.**

DATE	HIGH
9 Dec	320
15 Dec	195
14 Jan	144
15 Feb	120
15 Mar	104
14 Apr	37
15 May	50
15 Jun	31

let alone bought VA Linux myself (at $33 per share). But there's an important lesson here: Never buy a stock based on hype, especially when the hype has warped the price so drastically.

THE DO-IT-YOURSELF MENTALITY

Despite their abysmal performance, the market still overvalues a stable of stalwarts and a handful of hot young things. The key to winning in the stock market is to use this bias to your advantage. Keep an eye out for promising newcomers or temporarily out-of-favor winners, put your money in when everyone else is down on them or before the Street notices their worth, and you can reap huge rewards.

How do you do it? Very simple: You rely on your *own* calculations, not the latest "Top-10 Picks of the Year" from some national magazine. This strategy demands a little number crunching, but the math isn't that hard.

This chapter is all about getting the basics down. As an analyst, I spend about 70 hours a week working the numbers and picking apart the data. The portfolio manager who runs your mutual fund, the investment guru you saw on *Bloomberg,* even the author of that article on the "Top-10 Picks of the Year" all received guidance from me, or from other analysts, to help come up with a roster of stocks.

I get a lot of attention for doing what I do, but the truth is that you don't need to be an analyst to run the numbers. You don't even need to be that good in math. With the Web, basic information is available to anyone; you just need to know what to do with it. If you're ready to learn, I'm ready to teach. Here's Theory 1 from Mike's bag of analyzing tricks.

LOOK FORWARD

There are lots of ways to determine the value of a stock. But the big boy's baseline is the price-to-earnings (P/E) ratio. The P/E ratio is P (the current *price* of the stock) divided by E (one year's *earnings* per share). Simple enough, right? But here's where it gets sticky: You can find the P/E ratio listed in the business section of most major newspapers, but the E these papers (and most people) use is *last year's* earnings per share. That might be fine for your average blue-chip behemoth, but this book targets high-growth companies. High-growth companies need to be looking forward to stay on top, and so should you. I want you to make E *next year's* earnings per share (we'll refer to this as *four-quarter forward earnings*) so that you are always looking forward exactly one year.

E

This is *earnings,* the *E* in P/E. For high-tech companies, use *next year's* earnings per share—or, even better, the sum of the next four unreported quarters. Find it online at www.fool.com or at brokerage sites like e-Trade. It's normally listed as *consensus earnings estimate.*

In my mind, a company's value should always be judged based on its future prospects, not its past performance. For example, let's say you're thinking of investing in a company that made $5.00 a share last year. It sounds like a good bet until you find out that a competitor is about to release a product that is likely to bankrupt the company within a year. Basing your evaluation on last year's earnings now seems ludicrous, and yet that's precisely what most investors do. Remember: The future is more important than the past.

Companies with years of success under their belts get considerable consideration from investors. In fact, they get so much consideration that they're often extremely overvalued. They're deemed the Cadillacs of the stock market, and make no mistake, you'll pay through the nose for that Cadillac. What's interesting is that there may be a less known car sitting in the lot with precisely the same performance and future prospects. In fact, many companies that the average investor has never even heard of can give that fancy Cadillac a run for its money (and yours).

Scenario 1

To help you understand the way this works, I've come up with an example. Let's say there are two companies—call them Company A and Company B. You've got some money burning a hole in your pocket and you decide to invest it instead of buying a Rolex. But you just can't decide where to invest it; these two companies have caught your eye.

Year 1 has just ended, and Company A and Company B each earned $1.00 per share. Company A is a high-growth company expected to grow 100 percent in Year 2 and continue at a very high rate thereafter. Company B is a mature company—it's growing at about 5 percent per year and will probably continue in that range. If Company A's stock is trading at $50 per share and Company B's is trading at $25 per share, which one should you own?

Let's look at their P/E ratios. If we look backward, Company A's P/E is 50 and Company B's is 25. In other words, Company A appears twice as expensive, since both companies had the same earnings last year. Trusting the P/E from most newspapers, backward thinking might tip the scales in Company B's favor despite its lower growth rate, but with a quick jaunt to your favorite online resource (e-Trade, Schwab, or the Motley Fool), you'd unearth what you need for our forward-thinking approach.

Note: Remember, the *E* in our P/E is *next year's* expected earnings per share. The best number to use for this E is the *consensus earnings estimate*, which you can get from most online broker or financial sites. The consensus earnings estimate averages the forecasts for next year of all the analysts following the stock.

Let's assume that the consensus estimate for Company A's earnings next year is $2.00 per share, because Company A is expected to grow 100 percent. Company B is expected to grow 5 percent each year, so we'll assume that the consensus estimate for Company B's Year 2 earnings is $1.05. Using those numbers, the P/E based on forward earnings would be 25 for Company A and 24 for Company B (see Figure 9.3).

So, looking forward instead of backward, both companies have about the same P/E, yet Company A is growing 20 times

FIGURE 9.3   FORWARD AND BACKWARD P/E
CALCULATIONS.

STOCK	BACKWARD P/E	FORWARD P/E
Company A	$\dfrac{\$50}{\$1.00} = 50$	$\dfrac{\$50}{\$2.00} = 25$
Company B	$\dfrac{\$25}{\$1.00} = 25$	$\dfrac{\$25}{\$1.05} = 24$

faster. Suddenly, Company A doesn't seem so expensive. Just how good a deal is it? Take a look. In year 2, you'll fall behind about $1 per share in earnings by hitching your wagon to Company B, rather than Company A, but assuming that Company A's growth shrinks by about 10 percent a year (about average), the difference in earnings per share between the companies is more than $12 a mere five years out (see Figure 9.4). Suddenly, it's Company B that looks expensive. Looking forward, it's *worth* paying a rather large premium for Company A now.

Scenario 2

Now for a real live example. I've been hip on Dell for a number of years. The choice seems obvious now. Dell was the best performing stock of the 1990s, with an average compound annual return of 97.3

FIGURE 9.4   EARNINGS PER SHARE OVER
FIVE YEARS.

	EARNINGS PER SHARE			
STOCK	YEAR 2	YEAR 3	YEAR 4	YEAR 5
Company A	$2.00	$4.00	$7.60	$13.68
Company B	$1.05	$1.10	$1.16	$1.22

percent; a $2,000 investment 10 years ago would have become almost $1.8 million on January 1, 2000. The company has a lofty stock price to show for it, too. But the truth is, a few years back Dell's P/E didn't reflect the company's strength. Dell was growing its revenue at 50 percent per year and its earnings even more rapidly, while the S&P 500 was growing at only about 10 percent per year. In other words, Dell had at least five times the growth rate of the S&P 500. However, despite the numbers, most investors weren't biting. Dell was trading at a *lower* P/E than the S&P 500, even though it was worth at least twice as much. For many years, Dell was trading cheap.

Compare that to IBM (one of the Nifty 50, by the way). Big Blue was struggling to even *match* the S&P, let alone pass it, but it was trading at a high P/E. Despite its name recognition, IBM was an extremely poor investment.

Since it's a bit of a pain to go through the calculations each and every time, I've come up with a table to use as a rule of thumb for determining how much of a premium you should be willing to pay for various rates of growth versus the 10 percent S&P average. The chart also shows how this growth translates to different P/Es, based on the fact that the current average P/E for the S&P 500 is around 30 (see Figure 9.5). As you read this, the S&P P/E will probably be different from 30—that's why I've included a column for when the S&P P/E is 25. The last column tells you what percent higher than the S&P P/E each growth rate warrants. For example, a company with 20 percent growth should trade at about a 39 percent premium to the S&P. If the S&P P/E is 40, that company should trade at a P/E of 55.6 [(40 × 39%) + 40].

Remember, the table is meant to be used only as a guideline. No company will consistently perform in an "average" way. In addition to the table, make sure you weigh the management team, any competitive advantage or lack thereof, and the other qualitative factors discussed earlier in this book. For example, if a company is growing revenue at 60 percent, and the S&P P/E is 25, then an "expected P/E" for that company, as shown in Figure 9.5, would be 70.9. This applies to companies that are already earning a relatively "normal" amount for their business (we'll discuss what to do when this is not the case later on).

FIGURE 9.5   BALLPARK P/Es FOR COMPANIES WITH
VARIOUS RATES OF GROWTH.

GROWTH RATE	EXPECTED P/E		
	S&P P/E = 25	S&P P/E = 30	PREMIUM TO S&P P/E
10%	25.0	30.0	0%
20	34.7	41.7	39
30	44.9	53.9	80
40	53.9	64.7	116
50	62.2	74.7	149
60	70.9	85.1	184
80	91.9	110.3	268
100	100.8	121.0	303
150	181.8	218.2	627
200	239.5	287.4	858

Scenario 3

At this writing, Gateway Computer is trading at $57.50 per share, with a consensus earnings estim: te for 2000 of $1.83 per share. Gateway is growing at about 20 percent, but its P/E is 31 ($57.50/$1.83).

According to Figure 9.5, when the S&P average P/E is 30, a company with 20 percent growth should have a P/E of 41.7, about 39 percent more than the S&P 500. (If all of this seems confusing, take a look at Figure 9.6. It demonstrates how to calculate the P/E of 41.7 by using the S&P premium column. While this is obviously more involved than just reading the number off the chart, it shows the extra steps you need to use when the S&P P/E differs from 30.) With this in mind, Gateway should be trading at a P/E closer to 42. The company appears to be undervalued by about 30 percent.

FIGURE 9.6   CALCULATING GATEWAY'S P/E FROM THE S&P PREMIUM.

GROWTH RATE	EXPECTED P/E	P/E PREMIUM 10% GROWTH
10%	30.0	0%
20%	41.7	39%

S&P P/E × P/E premium = P/E premium 30 × 39% = 11.7
S&P P/E + P/E premium = expected Gateway P/E 30 + 11.7 = 41.7
Expected P/E × estimated earnings per share (EPS) = expected stock price 41.7 × 1.83 = 76.3
Current Gateway stock price = 57.5 Undervaluation = 33%

If you were considering investing in Gateway, it would be important to weigh all of these facts. If you believed that the other elements were strong, the company would be worth considering, especially during the dip.

LOOK FAST FORWARD

Hopefully, you've got a handle on forward thinking. Assuming you're still with me and aren't cursing my name, we're ready for Theory 2—what I like to call *fast-forward thinking.*

As you read this sentence, dozens of new companies are opening their doors. Some will make their founders and stockholders rich; others will have gone under before you've finished this sentence. With tons of new start-ups crowding the market, misinformation is rampant. The value of a stock should be based on three things and three things only:

- The expected growth rate of the company
- The consensus earnings estimate
- The degree of risk associated with the company's future prospects

The good news is that, unlike hype, the numbers don't lie. The bad news is that, with new companies, it's often impossible to calculate the P/E ratio. This is because there is *no E!* These companies have no earnings yet.

So forget P/E. It can't be done. For *really* new companies, forward thinking isn't forward enough. It's time to go into overdrive. With extremely young companies, you need to come up with a *fast* forward-thinking number. The Big Bertha of this calculation is called *market capitalization,* or *market cap.*

Think of the market cap as the value of a company. In the same way that the value of your stock is the current price of each share times the number of shares you own, the value of a company is the price of each share times the number of shares that the company has. It's really exactly the same thing.

You can easily find out how many shares a company has (from an annual report, online, or by calling the company directly). Once you've multiplied that number by the current stock price, you've got your market cap number. It's time for the price-to-revenue (P/R) ratio.

$$\text{P/E ratio} = \frac{\text{stock price}}{\text{earnings per share}}$$

$$\text{P/R ratio} = \frac{\text{market cap}}{\text{consensus forecast revenue}}$$

As mentioned, determining P/R is not that different from determining P/E. Since there are no earnings, now it's *revenue* that matters. With P/E you took the price of the stock and divided it by the earnings per share; here you take the market cap and divide it by the consensus forecast revenue. This, just like the consensus earnings estimate from the forward-thinking P/E, can be obtained from most financial Web sites. Remember, you can't use the consensus earnings estimate because there are no earnings, so you use the consensus forecast revenue, which is an average of the forecasts for next year's *revenue* made by all the analysts who follow the stock.

Scenario

As usual, we're going to compare Company A and Company B. Let's say Company A is an entity that's been around for awhile (in Internet years it's ancient, but in calendar years that means maybe two or three years old), and Company B is a newcomer as yet untested. Now, suppose the consensus forecast revenue for Company A is $30 million. Revenue is expected to grow at about 100 percent per year, and Company A's market cap is $300 million. This means that Company A's price-to-revenue ratio is 10. (To refresh: Take the $300 million market cap and divide it by the $30 million in consensus forecast revenue.) Company B is growing at the same rate as Company A and is in essentially the same business, but its revenue is forecast at $50 million. As a potential investor in both companies, what this means to you is this: In order to be as good an investment as Company A, Company B should have a price-to-revenue ratio of 10 as well. In order for this to be the case, Company B would need a market cap of $500 million (10 times next year's expected revenue of $50 million).

Company A's consensus forecast: $30 million.

Company B's consensus forecast: $50 million.

P/R for Company A:

$$\frac{\text{Market capitalization}}{\text{Consensus forecast}} = \frac{\$300 \text{ million}}{\$30 \text{ million}} = 10$$

Market cap for Company B: If Company B is comparable to Company A (similar growth in revenue and similar earnings opportunity), then its market cap can be calculated as follows:

$$\text{A's P/R} \times \text{B's forecast} = 10 \times \$50 \text{ million}$$
$$= \$500 \text{ million market cap}$$

This kind of backward calculation is often helpful when you're trying to establish the value of a new company. In this kind of situation, try to find a match for your newcomer, a more seasoned player. If you've got a software company, choose another software company. If it's a hardware company, match it to another hardware company, and so on. You want a company in the same business, with the same growth rate and similar prospects. The closer your match, the easier it is to figure out the value of the company you're dealing with. In the business this is known as finding the *comparable companies,* or *comps.*

A WORD OF WARNING

Companies that have yet to show earnings present a more risky investment. If you're intent on taking a gamble, hedge your bet by following these rules:

- Make sure these types of companies fill no more than two slots out of the seven in your portfolio.
- Find comparable companies in the same basic sector, with similar profit opportunities.
- Compare price to revenue.

This method is often used by investment banks trying to calculate how they should price the stock of a company they're taking public. (It assumes of course, that the comp is appropriately valued.) Before a big IPO, analysts like me work with investment bankers to establish a price, based on the price-to-revenue methodology. (For example, when my company took VA Linux public, we came up with a value for the stock based on a match with Cobalt, another Linux hardware company.)

P/R is used mostly for banking deals, but it can be applied just as readily to the average high-growth company already trading on the open market. Why not lift it for your own purposes?

EXTRA CREDIT

Finding good comparables helps when valuing young companies, but you can run into problems if all the comps happen to be temporary market darlings and therefore are overvalued. In this case, a second method can help ground you further. The method is known as calculating *earnings power* on forecast revenue.

To come up with this number, you'll need to find out a company's target model—the amount it expects to earn on each dollar in sales once it reaches maturity. You can glean this information by calling the company directly or by checking with a brokerage house that follows the stock.

For example, suppose a company's growth rate justifies a P/E of 120, but the company has no earnings. Further, suppose it is a software company that has targeted 20 percent as its eventual net profit level (the percentage of sales it earns after taxes). Then, it would eventually earn $20 on each $100 of revenue. Because it merits a 120 multiple of earnings, it would be worth $2,400 per $100 of revenue, or 24 times revenue, if it were mature. You need to ask two questions:

- Is the target model realistic?
- How much risk should be assigned in considering valuation?

The best way of assessing the first question is by looking at more mature companies that have similar operations—for example, what net margin levels do most software companies reach? The best way of assessing the second question is by trying to learn how much competition the company has and whether that competition has any competitive advantage. No matter what, some discount needs to be applied to account for the risk that the model might never be achieved. If the company is currently trading at 10 times revenue, it would certainly seem to be a good buy, but at 24 times revenue, maybe not so good.

When scouting for comps, it's important to find a good match. If you're feeling really diligent, find a few. The best way to look is by checking the Form 10-K or prospectus to see who the company itself considers to be its competitors. You can also just call up the company's investor relations department.

Once you've found some comps, compare the average P/R of these comparable companies to that of the newcomer you're considering. If the newcomer has a lower P/R than the basket of comparables and just as high a growth rate as their average (or higher), you've probably got a ringer. The newcomer is a good value.

HYPERGROWTH

The market has reached the point where some companies are going public before they even have *revenue*, let alone earnings. In these cases, you can't use P/E *or* P/R for valuation. Many pros will tell you that the benefit of investing so early is that you get in on the ground floor, which eventually will prove to be very valuable. My advice: Stay away.

SUMMING UP

- The value of a stock should be based on three things and three things only:

    1. The expected growth rate of the company

    2. The consensus earnings estimate

    3. The degree of risk associated with the company's future prospects

- Use a forward-thinking P/E ratio to calculate the value of high-growth companies that have earnings already. Use the P/R ratio to evaluate *really* new companies that have revenue but no earnings as yet. Pick at least one comp, and a basket of comps if possible, to see how the Street is valuing this type of entity on a P/R basis.

- Companies that have yet to show earnings are a higher risk. Don't let the newcomers occupy more than two slots on your roster of seven. Companies that can't be measured on a P/R basis should be ignored.

- Think prospectively, not reactively. The only way to avoid the pitfalls of overvaluation due to buzz is to do the math yourself and come up with your own valuation.

CHAPTER TEN

PICK ONLY HIGH-GROWTH COMPANIES

You are the general manager of a professional basketball team. It's 1984. You have the chance to draft Michael Jordan, but you'll have to trade three players to do it. Would you?

Well you'd be crazy not to. A player like that can transform a team's performance. A player like that is gold.

In stocks, as in basketball, you want to own Michael Jordan. You want the stock that's going to win the championship six out of seven years, not the one that ekes its way into the playoffs.

Superstars, whether stocks or players, bring up the general level of the entire team. Even if your other picks stink, with a superstar that averages 3,000 points per season bolstering them, there's still a chance of winning the game.

This is an important lesson. Every investor strives for a portfolio full of winners, but the truth is that you need only one or two superstars to achieve championship status.

Assembling a portfolio of stocks is much like assembling a starting lineup of players. Ideally, the entire team will be performing at slam-dunk capacity, but recruiting a few Michael Jordans doesn't hurt. Unfortunately, once Jordan has been in the league for five or

WHAT MAKES A SUPERSTAR STOCK?

- The company has revenue growth rate of 100 percent or more
- The company is a rookie with prospects—there's a strong likelihood that it will be highly profitable.

six years, he might be too expensive to acquire. By then, everybody will know what he's capable of, and getting Jordan on your team will mean blowing all the money you have to spend on just one player.

If you want a superstar, whether a stock or a player, it's best to get in early. That means betting on *prospects,* rather than performance. Rookies are riskier than old-timers, but they have a greater potential for superstar-level scoring.

I have a very simple philosophy when it comes to picking stocks for my portfolio: High growth is good. I want my portfolio to grow 25 percent or more per year, and in order for it to do so, the companies within it need to be growing *at least* that much—I prefer 30 to 40 percent for new investments. Not many companies can meet those numbers. The stocks that match the big tech score criteria are the best of the breed and usually are in the highest-growth sectors of the economy.

WHAT SPURS GROWTH?

When you're looking for stocks that you can hold for the long term, you should be looking for companies with long-term opportunities for revenue growth. There are three major factors that create this:

- The company is in a *market* that's growing rapidly.
- The company's *market share* is growing rapidly.
- The company creates new products or services that propel it into *new markets.*

If the company in question is in a market that's growing like wild-fire, I don't particularly care what its share is. If the market is growing only 10 percent a year, I do care. Why? I want companies that are growing revenue at a rate of 25 percent or more per year, and it's impossible for a company to grow its revenue 25 percent or more if it already has 85 percent of a slowly growing market.

Take Intel and Dell. Both are in the PC business, albeit different sectors. A few years back, I was urging all my friends to buy stock in Dell. It was a midget in a sea of giants—and one of those giants was Intel. People would say to me, "Mike, Intel has a monopoly, it has most of the market, and it's *cheaper.* Dell has a higher P/E! How in the world can you say I should buy Dell? Wouldn't you rather own Intel?"

I would reply, "No! Intel already *has* most of the market, so it's going to grow with the market. Dell has only a *tiny piece* of the market, and it's got a great business model. Mark my words, Dell is going to outgrow the market, and outgrow Intel."

It's not that you can *never* make money on a company in a slowly growing market; you can. Sometimes your company can grow quite a bit in a market that's growing slowly, but once it has the bulk of the market share, it's going to top out. The company is going to grow at the same (slow) speed as the market as a whole, unless it's able to branch out into new products.

Before investing in any company, try to find out how fast its market is growing. Call the company's investor relations department. Ask if there's an independent source you can check that follows market trends in the company's space. If the company's market is cell phones, find out how many cell phones are expected to be sold within the next few years. Find out what proportion of the population already has a cell phone. Find out if sales are beginning to level off.

Next, make a table for yourself. Write down how fast the market has grown in the past two years. Then record what share of the marketplace the company in question had two years ago, last year, and today. What share do you think they'll have three years from now? All of this should inform your decision of whether to invest (see Figure 10.1).

FIGURE 10.1   TRACKING MARKET GROWTH AND GROWTH IN MARKET SHARE.

PARAMETER	THIS YEAR	GROWTH RATE	NEXT YEAR
Total market sales	100 units	5%	105 units
Company's sales	90 units	17%	105 units
Company's market share	90%	11%	100%

For example, suppose a company has been growing as fast as the wind, in a market that's not going anywhere. It now has a 90 percent market share. Even if it captured the entire market next year, its revenue would still grow only 17 percent.

THE STOCKHOLDER SCREEN TEST

With so many stocks to choose from, it's hard to know which companies to add to your holdings. Forget the hype; focus on the numbers. I have a screen test that all companies (except a maximum of two promising rookies) should pass before being considered for your portfolio:

- The company has revenue of at least $100 million.
- The company's revenue has grown at least 25 percent each year for the past three years.
- The company's rate of growth decline does not exceed the rates listed in Figure 10.3, shown later in this chapter.

THE $100 MILLION MARK

The reason I prefer picking companies with $100 million or more of revenue is simple: I'm a chicken. I'm looking for the next Cisco, not the next bankruptcy. I don't want a highflyer that's here today, gone tomorrow. Don't get me wrong—I'm willing to invest in a great company that isn't showing any profits yet and probably won't for a long time, but I'm nervous about slapping down my money for a company with nothing going for it but well-placed hype. You should be, too. Once a company pulls in $100 million or more, it's clear you're dealing with more than smoke. That's why I like to use this number as a starting point.

REVENUE GROWTH OF AT LEAST 25 PERCENT FOR THREE YEARS RUNNING

A company's growth is an extremely important thing to look at before investing. However, lots of people get swayed by earnings growth. While it's nice when a stock goes up in price steadily each year, earnings growth can be a red herring, especially with younger companies.

In the early years, earnings growth can be astronomical, because the company keeps improving its business model. That's not a sustainable thing—you can't keep improving your business model forever. A company worth investing in for the long haul needs to be growing in *revenue,* and growing a lot.

My target in this book is to teach you how to make 25 percent or more on your stocks per year. With that in mind, you need to find companies that have *at least* 25 percent per year in revenue growth. In general, a company's stock goes up in relation to its revenue growth. As the company matures and becomes more profitable, its earnings growth will actually exceed its revenue growth—and its stock price can rise even faster.

I've used three years as a marker to help you differentiate a temporary (or cyclical) growth situation from a true growth company. A short-term event, like the Asian Crisis discussed in Chapter 3, can lead to misleading numbers. For example, in the midst of a crisis in Asia, a company's sales might drop drastically. Then, the company might show a temporary spike in revenue growth when conditions in Asia improve. Both changes are due to unusual circumstances, and not true fundamentals.

THE COMPAQ SAGA

I had a very positive call on Compaq in 1992. In fact, I had a very positive call on Compaq for most of the past decade. It was one of my favorite stocks from September 1992 to January 1998. At that time, Compaq made a very questionable decision: It bought Digital Equipment.

In my mind, this was a very bad sign. Despite its lofty stock price, and contrary to the general consensus, I decided that Compaq could no longer be a high-growth company.

Compaq, of course, disagreed. By late 1998 it was forecasting that its revenue would grow 17 percent during 1999. I was pretty skeptical. When I put the revenues of Compaq and Digital Equipment together, I realized that for the prior three years, the two companies had averaged a mere 6 percent per year in revenue growth. In fact, it was within a point of 6 percent each and every year. I published a report telling people to get out of the stock.

That was in December 1998. By February, Compaq had its tail between its legs. The company admitted that it wasn't going to meet the numbers it had promised—not a surprise to me, but a big surprise to the people who'd been taking Compaq at its word. Between the announcement and the end of the year, the stock slipped from over $50 a share to $18. Suddenly, I was interested.

At a sea-level $18, I thought it was a good time for investors to get back into the stock. Why? Because at its root, I believed in the company, and it had finally come back to earth. Compaq's estimates for 2000 placed growth at about 6 percent—the actual rate of its growth all along. Unlike the company's crazy estimate of 17 percent, I was comfortable with that.

The funny thing was, I found that most investors like to be lied to. The reason I say that is this: The year before, Compaq was a weak company with a bloated growth forecast, and everybody wanted in. In late 1999, it was a stronger company with a more realistic vision of its growth potential, and no one wanted to buy it. Investors were more comfortable with the stock when Compaq was lying! Because the new CEO refused to tell the public that Compaq would grow at some exaggerated rate, he had trouble getting investors on board.

GROWTH IS HARD TO MAINTAIN

When my kids were little, we used to have a growth chart tacked to the back of Danielle's bedroom door. Every few months, we'd line her and her brother up and mark off their progress with a pencil. I'm from a tall family, and my wife and I knew that both of our kids would be tall, but we were unprepared for the spurts and starts with which they reached their eventual stature.

In a way, high-growth companies are like high-growth kids. Investors, like parents, have a ballpark idea of what next year's growth will be, but surprises are almost inevitable. And while children grow at an astounding rate, their growth tapers off as they become more mature.

Similarly, as companies get older—and bigger—it's harder for them to grow as quickly. Think of it this way: Suppose you have a company with $100 million in revenue and it grows 100 percent. It's now a $200 million company. Year 2 rolls around and it grows only 80 percent. What happened?

Well, it's simple. In Year 1, the company needed to make only an additional $100 million in revenue to grow 100 percent. But in Year 2, as a $200 million company, to grow even 80 percent, it had to bring in revenue of *$360 million.* That's an extra $160 million in revenue, just to hit that 80 percent growth rate. This is a vital thing to keep in mind when you're looking at high-growth companies: The bigger you get, the harder it is to maintain revenue growth. When a mature company announces that it's expecting a jump in revenue growth the next year, be suspicious.

SCENARIO 1

Have you ever heard the parable of the emperor and the farmer? If so, bear with me. If not, there's no better time.

A farmer saves the emperor's life. The ruler says to the farmer, "I want to reward you in some way. I'm going to give you a million grains of rice—enough to feed your family for many years. You will be a wealthy man."

The farmer says, his head bowed, "Thank you for your kindness, but I am a simple man. Perhaps you will agree to this instead—I have a checkerboard with 64 squares. Instead of so many sacks of rice, could you do this? In the first week, give me one grain of rice for the first square of my checkerboard. The second week, give me two grains of rice for the second square. Then, each week thereafter, could you keep doubling the number of grains until all 64 squares are accounted for? I would prefer that, Your Highness."

Perhaps you think the farmer was stupid. Perhaps not. Let's see (see Figure 10.2).

Ahh, Grasshopper! Welcome to the law of doubling. Hopefully, you now understand why it's next to impossible for a company to keep on doubling its revenue each year—things get big *fast!* The "stupid" peasant has been granted more rice than exists in the world.

FIGURE 10.2   DOUBLING THE NUMBER OF GRAINS OF RICE ON EACH SQUARE OF A CHECKERBOARD.

POSITION	GRAINS OF RICE
Square 1	1
Square 8	128
Square 16	32,768
Square 32	2,147,483,648
Square 48	140,737,000,000,000
Square 64	9,223,372,037,000,000,000

RULE OF THUMB

So now you know what kind of growth is unreasonable. How much growth is *reasonable?* Well, the math required to do this from scratch is no cakewalk, so I've done some analysis and come up with a rough rule of thumb for you to use. If you're a glutton for punishment, you can try the mathematics yourself. Otherwise, this should suffice.

We're looking for unusual companies—companies growing by at least 25 percent per year. Let's estimate for our purposes that the average rate of growth for all S&P companies is 10 percent. This is the *mean.*

ROUGH RULE OF THUMB

Each year most companies' growth rates move toward the mean by about 17.5 percent of the difference, on average.

As you saw from Scenario 1, it's hard for companies to maintain rapid growth. In fact, a small decline is almost inevitable. The best companies will manage to slow their decline, the worst companies will slide more quickly, but on average, for growth companies, the rough rule of thumb proves pretty accurate.

If you're getting a sneaking suspicion that more math is on the horizon, you're right. The good news is that you can trust the following mean truth formula and plug your numbers right into it. Figure 10.3 also shows estimates for the average decline in growth of companies at various growth rates.

Amount of decline = current year's growth × rate of decline

Ballpark estimate of next year's growth =
current year's growth − amount of decline

In order to sort through all this mumbo jumbo, let's look at a scenario.

SCENARIO 2

A company's revenue is growing at 40 percent per year. Looking at Figure 10.3, note that the rate of decline for a company growing between 31 and 60 percent is 15 percent. Using the formula, you calculate:

Amount of decline = current year's growth × rate of decline

Amount of decline = 40% × 15% = 6%

Next year's growth = current year's growth − amount of decline

Next year's growth = 40% − 6% = 34%

For the company in question, you'd expect next year's growth to be about 34 percent. Regardless of what analysts are forecasting for this company, you should be thinking that next year's growth will be around 34 percent.

From February 1999 to February 2000, Dell did a pretty bad job of guiding the Street. It overpromised, and the press punished Dell with headlines shouting "Dell Barely Meets the Numbers."

FIGURE 10.3   DECLINE IN RATE OF GROWTH BASED ON CURRENT RATE OF GROWTH.

CURRENT GROWTH RATE, %	DECLINE IN GROWTH RATE, %
<11	0
11–20	5
21–30	10
31–60	15
61–100	20
101–200	25
≧200	30

Sun, in contrast, kept its guidance very conservative. During the same time period, it beat the numbers every quarter. Everywhere you looked, you read how great Sun was doing.

So how great *was* Sun doing? Almost all the investors I spoke to thought that Sun had done much better than Dell over the 12 months in question. The truth is that Dell's revenue growth was 38 percent and Sun's was 23 percent. Dell had grown almost 50 percent faster than Sun, but the headlines skewed the two companies' trading levels. In February 2000, Dell's P/E was around 40 and Sun's was around 95. The company with the lower growth rate had well over twice the P/E.

Now don't get me wrong—Sun is a fabulous company, but the numbers here just didn't make sense. As you can see from Figure 9.5, a company growing 25 percent per year should have a P/E between 35 and 45. Sun is just such a company, and it was trading at 95! Now it is possible that Sun will grow 50 percent or more, but for the past several years its growth rate has been holding fairly steady at 20 to 25 percent. Strangely, Wall Street is likely to continue to reward Sun's stock if the company keeps beating expectations and its growth holds firm or rises.

SCENARIO 3

Company A and Company B have perfectly matched histories. Last year they both had revenue growth rates of 40 percent; the year before, they had growth rates of 45 percent. Looking at these numbers and applying the rule of thumb, I would expect both companies to grow at about 34 percent next year. Remember, high growth rates decline toward the mean. Right now, both companies are growing 40 percent per year. The normal growth falloff for each would be 15 percent of those 40 points, or about 6 percent. I'd start by thinking that each of these companies should grow about 34 percent next year. They've grown at the same rate every year since they've both been in business, so barring some very unusual circumstances, such as a major new product release or a key hire, that would be my expectation. But remember, analysts are predicting that Company A will grow by 50 percent and Company B will drop down to 25 percent.

Let's assume that both companies made $1 per share last year, just to keep the math easy, and that earnings grow at the same rate as revenue. Recall that Company A has a P/E of 50. If analysts are predicting 50 percent growth, that means they're forecasting earnings of $1.50 per share for next year. And if Company B's forecast is for only 25 percent growth, that means $1.25 per share in earnings, with a P/E of 30. When we put the rule of thumb into action and plug in the 34 percent we came up with before, it becomes clear that if we're right, analysts have warped things. Because of their rosy outlook, Company A is trading at $75.00 a share, while Company B is trading at $37.50. As mentioned before, I expect both companies to have similar growth for next year, and when we put our own numbers into play they're quite at odds with industry predictions. Both companies should be trading at a P/E of 40, or $54 per share. That makes Company A over-valued by more than $20.00 and Company B a steal at $37.50 (see Figure 10.4).

FIGURE 10.4   WALL STREET'S ANALYSIS VERSUS MIKE'S ANALYSIS.

What Wall Street Is Saying					
STOCK	**EPS LAST YEAR**	**EXPECTED GROWTH**	**FORECAST EPS NEXT YEAR**	**P/E**	**STOCK PRICE**
Company A	$1.00	50%	$1.50	50	$75.00
Company B	$1.00	25%	$1.25	30	$37.50

What Mike Thinks					
STOCK	**EPS LAST YEAR**	**EXPECTED GROWTH**	**FORECAST EPS NEXT YEAR**	**P/E**	**REALISTIC STOCK PRICE**
Company A	$1.00	35%	$1.34	40	$53.60
Company B	$1.00	35%	$1.34	40	$53.60

The only weakness in this equation is that it doesn't take incremental events into account. If you're aware of some big tragedy or triumph coming down the pipe, take that 34 percent with a grain of salt.

Remember, these calculations are estimates for an average result. Almost *no* company will be average. Always expect variations from the rule, but be skeptical when those variations seem widely out of line. Whittle out the company's reasoning for predicting unprecedented growth, and decide if you believe it.

What I've finally realized, after a lot of years on Wall Street, is that one company's prognosis versus that of another often has more to do with a speech from an overly optimistic CEO than it does with anything else. No problem—the rule of thumb takes analyst optimism or pessimism out of the equation. You don't have to take the pros' word for anything.

SUMMING UP

- Focus your portfolio on companies that have revenue growth of at least 25 percent per year.

- As companies become more mature, high growth is harder to maintain.

- Each year, most companies' growth rates move toward the mean (10 percent) by about 17.5 percent of the difference.

- Remember the mean truth formula:

Amount of decline =
current year's growth × rate of decline

Ballpark estimate of next year's growth =
current year's growth − amount of decline

- Long-term revenue growth is spurred by three major factors:

  1. The company is in a *market* that's growing rapidly.

  2. The company's *market share* is growing rapidly.

  3. The company creates new products or services that propel it into *new markets*.

- Aside from rookies with the potential to be superstars, any stock you place in your portfolio should pass the three-part stockholder screen test:

    1. The company has revenue of at least $100 million.

    2. The company's revenue has grown at least 25 percent each year for the past three years.

    3. The company's rate of growth decline does not exceed the rates identified as reasonable in Figure 10.3.

- Rookies should be growing by over 100 percent per year, even if they have yet to show profits.

CHAPTER ELEVEN

THE BEST STOCKS ARE CHEAPER THAN YOU THINK

Fortune magazine once called me a genius. I got a lot of phone calls that month. Journalists, portfolio managers, long-lost friends—everybody wanted to pick my brain about the next big thing.

It's pretty cool to be treated for awhile as if you've been handed the word of God regarding which stocks are going to hit and which are going to go under (not to say that God doesn't have anything better to do than watch the market). But the truth is, genius or no genius, guru or no guru, *no* industry expert knows for sure, in advance, how well a company's going to do. Even the *company itself* doesn't know.

As far as I'm concerned, believing otherwise is one of the most widely held misconceptions about the stock market. It couldn't be further from the truth. Neither analysts nor CEOs can accurately predict next year's revenues or earnings. As a company becomes more mature, management can sometimes make a pretty good guess—but it's only a guess. Even a Coca-Cola or a Motorola can radically miscalculate from time to time.

When you're looking at analyst predictions on some Web site, or expert advice in a magazine, remember this: You know that phrase, "Your guess is as good as mine"? Take it to heart. Many professional investors don't know much more than you do. They may even know less. According to the Motley Fool, more than 75 percent of all mutual funds underperform the market's average return each year. You can do better.

Why are the numbers so drastic? It's the lemming phenomenon. Some of these so-called experts do nothing more than mimic what a company is spouting will come to pass.

If you've ever played Monopoly, you know that different players approach risk in different ways. Some hoard, some cheat, some are made virtually impotent by paranoia, while others go off half-cocked. In business, as in Monopoly, no one can accurately predict who will win ahead of time. But while companies have no idea in advance what the next quarter's results will be, they each have specific strategies for how to play the game.

THE GAME

This is how it works. Each quarter, analysts attempt to do the impossible. They are charged with predicting, in advance, how much a company will earn. These crystal-ball analyses are averaged out and lumped together in a number called the *consensus earnings estimate*. It is the basis for many Wall Street investment decisions.

As mentioned, company fortune telling is a tricky business, and getting it right can make or break an analyst's reputation. To help the analysts along, most companies host conference calls and hold meetings to discuss what they believe the future will hold for them and to keep analysts abreast of the issues that could affect the quarter.

Analysts consider what said companies tell them, run the numbers, and come to a decision as to what they believe will come to pass. Portfolio managers and other institutional investors then quiz their favorite analysts about their favorite companies and any potential quarter trouble spots. They decide who to believe. Everyone places their bets. And then, at the end of the quarter, the moment of truth arrives.

As you can see, the analyst's role in this dance is that of independent observer. Ideally, what analysts do is what their name implies—they analyze the situation. Good analysts routinely visit the companies they follow to talk to management. They follow industry trends like a hawk. They speak to customers and suppliers, keep track of revenue, and do detailed financial modeling. Then they factor all of these things into their quarterly predictions.

Unfortunately, many analysts don't go to all that trouble. Instead, they rely on what's called *guidance*. As a big part of any analyst's job is to guess next quarter's earnings per share (EPS) for each of the companies he or she follows, companies provide analysts with advice, or guidance. A good analyst factors guidance into his or her model. A lazy one uses it verbatim.

For example, a company's CFO might say to a group of analysts, "We think we can do $10 billion in revenue." Some analysts will take them at their word and plug that number directly into their models, without considering the mitigating factors that could set the company off course. A company's CFO might tell a group of analysts, "Last year we grew 40 percent and we think we can maintain that range," and some "experts" will trust them blindly.

A company's CFO might even say, "The analyst consensus right now is that we're going to do between 38 and 42 percent growth next year, and we're comfortable with that." There have been times when a company has said something along those lines and I've looked at the numbers and realized that not a single analyst was in that range at the time of the announcement. Such companies are feeding analysts the numbers while pretending that they were arrived at independently. They want to tell analysts what to do without having officially told them.

Lots of analysts are only too happy to oblige. Within a week or two many have changed their forecasts to toe the company line. It seems that on Wall Street you can lead a horse to water *and* make it drink.

This blind dependence on company predictions irks me to no end. Analysts get paid big bucks to analyze, not to regurgitate. That's their job. I believe an analyst should know a product's potential even better than the company does. I believe that a good analyst should be able to predict a company's earnings for the next year even more accurately than its CEO. Unfortunately, quite a few merely parrot the company's top management.

I tell you this not to toot my own horn or to bad-mouth my cohorts, but because I want you to understand how professional forecasts come about. They are not gospel. While it's a good idea to take a look at analyst reports and company forecasts, they don't tell the whole story. They can tell you a lot, and any information you can glean on a company is worth looking at, but please, look with a critical eye. Don't accept everything you read without questioning it. Questioning is important.

SCENARIO 1

Last year Company A and Company B both earned $1 per share and had revenue growth of 60 percent. The year before they both had revenue growth of 70 percent. In fact, amazingly enough, their histories exactly match. They have had the same revenue growth forever. On January 1 of the new year, analysts predict that Company A will have 65 percent revenue growth next year, and also predict that Company B's revenue growth will drop to 25 percent. Company A is currently trading at a P/E of 60, and Company B is trading at a P/E of 30 (see Figure 11.1). What should you be thinking as an investor?

My bet is that most investors would favor Company A; people like a rosy outlook. They like to hear that a company's growth rate is going to go up. Guess what? Most investors would be wrong. Unless there is evidence of something really radical on Company A's horizon, you should buy Company B.

The sad truth is that success is hard to maintain. Even with high-growth companies, revenue rates typically decline a bit each

FIGURE 11.1   COMPARING COMPANY A AND COMPANY B.

STOCK	EPS LAST YEAR	EXPECTED GROWTH	FORECAST EPS NEXT YEAR	CURRENT P/E	STOCK PRICE
Company A	$1.00	65%	$1.65	60	$99.00
Company B	$1.00	25%	$1.25	30	$37.50

year. To me, Company A's numbers look suspicious, and Company B looks like a bargain.

Why do I favor Company B? Because going from 60 to 25 percent is a pretty big drop. It gets to my gut. I just don't believe it. I think Company B probably told analysts that its earnings were going to be low and the analysts listened. My hunch is that Company B understands the Wall Street game and knows that you're supposed to beat the numbers you feed analysts at the beginning of the year. With that in mind, it lowballed.

Company A, on the other hand, seems overly optimistic. Just like Company B, it's had a decline in its rate of revenue growth each year for the past two years. Unless there's something big coming down the pipe (a new product, a strategic partnership, etc.) there's no reason to expect this to change. It appears to me that Company A is looking through rose-colored glasses and that analysts are taking the company at its word.

Suspicion? Gut reactions? Hunches? What is this, the psychic network? Well, no, but what I want you to take out of Scenario 1 is this: Predicting a stock's performance for the next year is not an exact science. There are, however, a few things that should set off a warning bell in your head. One of them is when a company forecasts a huge jump (or fall) in revenue. Be very skeptical of that.

DON'T BELIEVE EVERYTHING YOU READ

Guidance is serious business. Ten years ago, results were what mattered. How well a company performed determined the rise and fall of its shares. These days, many investors seem to care more about how well a company's results match Wall Street's expectations than they do about the results themselves.

Every analyst following a company at least partially bases his or her earning estimates on guidance. In a perfect world, such direction would result in consensus estimates that had an equal chance of exceeding or falling short of actual results. We don't live in a perfect world. In reality, what will ultimately happen in any given quarter is a mystery—and some managements are consistently optimistic, some are consistently conservative, and some are consistently inconsistent.

CONSENSUS EARNINGS ESTIMATE

Consensus is the average of all analysts' predictions for a company's future estimated earnings per share (EPS).

If a company usually errs in one direction (which in turn causes consensus to err in the same direction), it has what I call a *guidance bias*. I consider bias to be positive if the company consistently beats estimates, negative if it consistently falls short. Most people ignore guidance track records when making stock decisions, but you should take them very seriously. Once you understand how it works, you'd be a fool not to factor bias into your buying decisions.

SCENARIO 2

Suppose Company A's earnings are growing 10 percent per year and Company B's are growing 50 percent per year. Company A's stock is at $44 and Company B's is at $75, and both companies earned $2.00 per share in 1999. With this in mind, P/E calculated on forward consensus EPS would yield a multiple, or P/E, of 20 for Company A and a multiple of 25 for Company B (see Figures 11.2 and 11.3).

FIGURE 11.2   GROWTH COMPANY P/E MULTIPLES.

PARAMETER	COMPANY A	COMPANY B
Price	$44.00	$75.00
1998 EPS	$2.00	$2.00
1999 EPS	$2.20	$3.00
Expected growth	10%	50%
Backward multiple	22	38
Forward multiple	20	25

FIGURE 11.3   CALCULATING P/E AND FORWARD P/E.

COMPANY A
$P/E = \dfrac{\$44.00}{\$2.00} = 22 \qquad \text{Forward P/E} = \dfrac{\$44.00}{\$2.20} = 20$

COMPANY B
$P/E = \dfrac{\$75.00}{\$2.00} = 38 \qquad \text{Forward P/E} = \dfrac{\$75.00}{\$3.00} = 25$

Now, suppose Company A has no guidance bias, but Company B's actual results consistently exceed expectations by 25 percent. If we adjust Company B's forecast earnings by the 25 percent guidance bias, our E would be \$3.75 rather than \$3.00 [\$3.00 + (\$3.00 × 25%)]. Then, while the perceived forward P/E for Company B is 25, the adjusted P/E is 20 (see Figure 11.3). Or, to put it another way, both Company A and Company B have the same *equivalent P/E* (EP/E)—a forward P/E adjusted for guidance bias.

Now think about this. Using the historical P/E valuation, Company B has a multiple of 38 versus 22 for Company A. But looking forward and adjusting for guidance bias yields the same multiple of 20 for both (see Figure 11.4). Assuming that there are no anomalies here, Company B, at five times the growth rate, isn't nearly as expensive as it appears. In fact, it's a far *cheaper* stock.

FIGURE 11.4   FORWARD VERSUS EQUIVALENT P/E MULTIPLES.

STOCK	FORWARD MULTIPLE	GUIDANCE BIAS	EQUIVALENT MULTIPLE
Company A	20	0%	20
Company B	25	25%	20

APPLYING GUIDANCE BIAS
TO VALUATION

Analysts rely on company guidance. It helps them form their earnings estimates. At the same time, companies are under tremendous pressure to provide a number that's achievable—without knowing in advance where that quarter's unexpected dangers lie.

How companies handle this unpredictability is what sets them apart. Some companies are conservative in the guidance they give analysts, quarter after quarter, beating the numbers each and every time. Others give optimistic guidance, then consistently come up short. Those that routinely exceed the consensus estimates have a *positive* guidance bias, and those that consistently miss the boat have a *negative* one. Other companies have no bias at all. For example, for years Procter & Gamble and General Electric consistently came in right on the money—offering guidance each quarter that typically came within 1 percent of actual earnings. (In recent quarters, they have been less consistent.)

EXPENSIVE STOCKS THAT ARE ACTUALLY CHEAP

An important thing to remember is that companies with high guidance bias often appear overvalued because investors, at least partly, use consensus numbers to calculate their forward P/E ratio. In November 1998, for example, Microsoft's multiple was 42 times calendar 1999 EPS estimates, while Compaq appeared far cheaper with a P/E of 18 (see Figure 11.5).

However, if one applied historical guidance bias, Microsoft's adjusted multiple shrank to 34, while Compaq's was elevated to 22. Even if one assumed that the biases, both positive and negative, would moderate, the gap still closes dramatically. The decision regarding which stock is a better value certainly shifts once these adjustments are made.

SCENARIO 3

Time for another example. It's November 1998. You're considering buying stock in Compaq. A friend of yours recommends that

**FIGURE 11.5   EQUIVALENT CALENDAR YEAR 1999
P/E RATIOS.**

COMPANY	P/E	GUIDANCE BIAS	EQUIVALENT P/E	ADJUSTED BIAS*	ADJUSTED EP/E
Microsoft	42	25%	34	20%	35
Compaq	18	−20%	22	−10%	20

*Assumes moderation of bias.
Note: Stock prices as of November 3, 1998.

you look at Dell instead, but Dell's P/E, based on consensus 1999 earnings estimates, is a whopping 44, whereas Compaq's forward P/E is only 20. You pat yourself on the back for ignoring what's in vogue and buy Compaq.

What you've failed to take into account is the fact that the *E* in both companies' P/E ratios is based on their own earnings guidance and that Dell is traditionally cautious and Compaq is overly optimistic. In fact, from 1996 to 1998, Dell's actual earnings averaged 63 percent higher than its guidance, while Compaq had negative guidance bias—consistently missing numbers by 20 percent. If the trend continues, then factoring in their biases, Dell's real 1999 P/E (or equivalent P/E) isn't 44, it's 27. And Compaq's is 24, not 20. Dell may still be a bit more expensive, but not as expensive as it first appeared. With its rapid-fire growth rate, it is probably worth the three-point premium over problem-laden Compaq (see Figure 11.6).

I first began incorporating guidance bias into my earnings estimates in earnest in late 1996. I calculated guidance bias, EP/E, and EP/E to growth for several high-tech companies. Then I took some well-known companies in areas other than technology—Coca-Cola, Gillette, Kellogg's, and Wal-Mart—which I'll hereafter refer to as the *consumer group.*

I noticed that despite investor confidence that these companies were safe stocks, the consumer group's performance consistently fell short of expectations.

FIGURE 11.6   ACTUAL EARNINGS VERSUS GUIDANCE.

COMPANY	GUIDANCE BIAS*	EQUIVALENT 1999 P/E	CONSENSUS 1999 P/E	PRICE†	1-YEAR RETURN
Consistently Positive					
Dell	63%	27	44	$64	200%
Microsoft	25%	35	43	$110	64%
Gap	22%	24	30	$68	86%
Inconsistent					
Coca-Cola	−9%	49	45	$71	14%
Compaq	−20%	24	20	$34	−10%
Consistently Negative					
Kellogg's	−29%	33	23	$34	−25%
JCPenney	−40%	24	14	$51	−22%
Motorola	−56%	70	31	$58	−10%

*Average historical difference between actual earnings and consensus estimates 15 months prior to earnings announcement.
†As of November 1998.

The companies in the group failed to learn from their guidance mistakes. Negative guidance bias continued. From 1996 through 1999, the consumer group companies showed an average guidance bias of roughly −11% (see Figure 11.7). This placed their EP/E average at 37. Because the group's revenue growth was only 4 percent, EP/E to growth of each and every one of them was four or more times Dell's ratio, and at least twice that of Microsoft's (excluding the adjustments for Microsoft's conservative accounting). The consumer group was full of popular companies that were bad investments.

FIGURE 11.7 **CONSUMER GROUP EQUIVALENT**
CALENDAR YEAR 1999 P/E RATIOS.

COMPANY	REVENUE GROWTH	P/E	GUIDANCE BIAS	EQUIVALENT P/E	EP/E TO GROWTH
Wal-Mart	13%	31	−1%	31	2.36
Gillette	4	34	−5	35	8.00
Coca-Cola	0	46	−9	50	NA
Kellogg's	−1	23	−29	33	NA
Average	4%	33	−11%	37	
S&P 500	4%	23	1%	23	5.68

CALCULATING QUARTERLY GUIDANCE BIAS

Instead of predicting earnings for a total year, I like to treat things quarter by quarter. This is important for high-growth companies in particular, as growth can vary by hundreds of percentage points. It's also important because it helps to pick up changes in momentum that require adjustments in expectations. Finally, it's important because certain trends in revenue have to do with long-term issues, while others are based on seasonality.

For example, if a company is in the consumer space, revenue can get a huge boost during December (Christmas shopping) or September (new school year), but may fall off significantly after the holiday buying spree.

If you look at a consumer company like Amazon and notice that December revenue growth has been around 30 percent for the past three years, and the company's guidance this year places it at 10 to 12 percent, it's important to question that conservatism. Why would this Christmas be any different than the ones before it? In the same vein, when looking at a company's yearly performance, you may notice that growth goes from 20 percent in Year 1, to 15 percent in

Year 2, to 10 percent in Year 3. If the company's Year 4 estimate is a sky-high 20 percent, be suspicious. Looking at the trend line, it's unlikely that the company will squeak by with 10 percent growth, let alone reach 20%. Laying things out by quarter helps you decide how to weigh a company's guidance.

To forecast the next quarter, look at the past 12 quarters and create a table to display growth sequentially. Don't place the 12 quarters in a line. Place each year's quarters in a column and then line them up to face each year's equivalent quarters (see Figure 11.8). This will allow you to observe both yearly and seasonal trend lines.

Next, it's time to determine sequential growth. After you've done so, place your calculations next to the appropriate quarter in the table.

$$\text{Sequential growth} = \frac{\text{revenue this quarter}}{\text{revenue previous quarter}} - 1$$

For example, suppose Company A had $80 million in revenue in the September 1999 quarter and $100 million in the December quarter. The December quarter sequential growth is calculated as follows*:

$$\text{December sequential growth} = \frac{\text{December revenue}}{\text{September revenue}} - 1$$

$$= \frac{\$100 \text{ million}}{\$80 \text{ million}} - 1$$

$$= 1.25 - 1$$

$$= 0.25 \text{ or } 25\%$$

*If you're familiar with a spreadsheet program, like Excel, you can plug all the historical revenue numbers by quarter into a spreadsheet and set up formulas to do the sequential growth calculation for each quarter. The spreadsheet will do the rest.

FIGURE 11.8   LAYING OUT A TABLE TO DISPLAY
GROWTH BY QUARTERS.

1998 QUARTERS	1999 QUARTERS	2000 QUARTERS
March	March	March
June	June	June
September	September	September
December	December	December

When I calculate a revenue estimate for the next year, I first fill
in the quarterly sequential growth estimates. Let's say that for the
three previous March quarters, Company A had sequential growth
of 2 to 3 percent. I usually assume growth will slow in my models,
so I would take that 2 to 3 percent into account and estimate
March 2001 sequential growth at about 1 percent (see Figure
11.9). I'd follow this with about 4, 8, and 24 percent sequential
growth in the following three quarters.

FIGURE 11.9   ESTIMATED QUARTERLY GROWTH
BASED ON THREE PREVIOUS
QUARTERS.

QUARTER	YEAR			
	1998	1999	2000	2001
March	2%	3%	2%	1%
June	8	7	5	4
September	13	12	10	8
December	28	26	25	24

Returning to the March quarter in question, I'd then use the formula given previously and calculate the March quarter revenue as equal to December revenue plus the 1 percent sequential growth.

$$\text{March revenue} = \text{December revenue} \times 1$$
$$+ \text{December revenue} \times 1\%$$

In other words:

$$\text{March revenue} = \text{December revenue} \times 1.01$$

If December revenue was \$100 million, this would make my March estimate \$101 million. In a similar manner, June quarter revenue would equal 1.04 times March quarter revenue; likewise, September = 1.08 × June, and December = 1.24 × September.

Hopefully, you're still with me. Calculating all of this can be time consuming. From a mathematical perspective, you are currently in the most difficult section of the book.

However, what this section teaches is worth learning. This method will give you insight as to whether a company's guidance for the quarter seems conservative or aggressive. That can put you way ahead of the pack, and even ahead of most Wall Street analysts. It's certainly served *me* well.

In fact, it was this very method that tipped me off in December 1998 to an unlikelihood regarding Compaq. The company had forecast a sequential revenue jump that substantially exceeded any December quarter in recent history and indicated that this unheard-of growth would be followed by a strong increase in the next quarter as well. After lining up the quarters, I was pretty suspicious. In fact, I was very suspicious. But I was probably the *only* suspicious analyst on Wall Street. I warned investors that the revenue jump was incredibly unlikely. I was right. The December quarter came in about \$400 million short of expectations.

WHY POSITIVE BIAS?

Many of today's most successful companies have learned the hard way that the ticket to a steady climb up the Nasdaq is consistently meeting or beating expectations. Because of this, the best-managed

FINDING THE FIGURES

I personally think that the easiest way to get revenue information is to look at a company's annual report. But I'm from the old school. You can also find information online at the following sites:

- *www.fool.com.* Click on Quotes and Data. Once there, look at *financials.*
- *www.yahoo.com.* Go to the Finance section. Look at the *analyst reports* and *SEC filings.*

entities tend to be conservative with their guidance. Remember: Management is aiming for consensus estimates (averages of EPS projections among analysts) that rise steadily over time, and it wants to report results each quarter that exceed those estimates.

No one has a crystal ball, but some management teams are more cautious than others in considering the future and what it will mean to their bottom lines. To be honest, some are just plain paranoid. Should a growth company fail to meet expectations, its stock is likely to sell off heavily. The thought of that evidently keeps many a manager up at night.

THE DELL DILEMMA

Dell had a serious change in guidance bias during 1999 (Dell's fiscal 2000). Using quarterly sequential forecasting, I realized that it was being overly aggressive in its guidance—a huge change for a company known for its positive guidance bias. Struggling to meet those overly optimistic numbers each quarter hurt Dell's stock, even though its revenues were fairly good. Part of the problem was that Dell, which had defied the normal drop in growth for more than three years, began to experience more expected declines. Management refused to accept this. At this writing, it's not clear whether the company has returned to a conservative view.

Inasmuch as every quarter is filled with risk factors for a growth company (even if most are of low probability), reasons for cautious guidance always exist. Some companies take these risks extremely seriously. Some take them with a grain of salt.

There are also those that *pretend* to take them extremely seriously, while taking them with a grain of salt. Smart managers know that in order for the earnings they report at the end of the quarter to exceed consensus, they need to keep analyst expectations in check. To do so, they typically cry caution and attempt to steer analysts towards the low end of the EPS spectrum.

It's a fine balance. If the company lowballs too much, its guidance becomes suspect, and analysts who want to ensure accurate estimates tend to issue forecasts well above company guidance. Whether because of true paranoia or a steadfast intent to ensure a conservative consensus number, companies like Dell and Microsoft usually rally against suspicion by pulling out some convincing reason why a particular quarter is riskier than usual.

Lowballers give all kinds of justifications as to why there's reason for caution. Here are a few I seem to hear again and again. Although all of them are pretty slim risks, it's hard to dismiss a company that is intent on pushing them. I can't think of a single quarter in the past decade where they weren't at least a possibility.

- Some geographical region is running into an economic slowdown.
- Penetration levels have peaked.
- Customers could decide to keep machines and software longer.
- Competitive issues could hurt prices and margins.

Because strong companies like Dell and Microsoft consistently underpredict, they're vulnerable to skepticism. One can cry wolf only so many times.

This skepticism often leads to what is known in the industry as the *whisper number.* The whisper number phenomenon is a direct result of guidance bias. When earnings reports exceed expectations, stock prices usually shoot up. For individual investors looking to buy said stock, this is irksome enough, but for institutional investors who purchase thousands of shares at a time, it can be a real problem.

As a company's earnings reporting date approaches, fund managers need to decide whether they should expect earnings to beat the consensus for the quarter. To do so, they often query analysts, asking them whether they think the real number will be higher or lower than the consensus.

It's an analyst's job to provide advice. Ideally, we analysts know the company better than anyone, and we do our best to answer questions along these lines. Analyst responses create an unpublished, rough, new consensus—the whisper number.

Because the whisper number is unpublished hearsay and arises when a company is in its quiet period, it's a loose cannon. It can affect movement in a stock even more than the published consensus number.

The whisper number is an elusive thing. A fund manager might tell analysts that he or she hears that Microsoft could beat the consensus by $0.10 or more. If my competitors and I repeat this whisper number when another manager asks us what we are hearing, it can become the expectation—even though it differs from the published consensus.

If the stock starts trading based on this higher expectation, and Microsoft then comes in at only $0.05 above the published consensus estimates, many investors will be disappointed and the stock might take a hit. It could even fall below the level it was at before expectations were "whispered up."

Virtually every portfolio manager's performance is measured quarterly, or even monthly, making it necessary for them to be focused on near-term performance. To get a bargain, portfolio managers need to buy shares before the company reports its earnings, and to prevent a disaster, they want to sell before a huge disappointment is officially announced. This is what makes this kind of hearsay so appealing.

Companies most subject to the whisper number are those that consistently report results exceeding consensus by a wide margin—companies like Dell and Microsoft. If they want to come in above the consensus (whether published or whisper), they need to prove that their guidance is worth something. They need to limit the unexpected. A company's best defense against an overzealous whisper number is the prevention of large upside surprises.

A WORD OF WARNING

Past bias is not a guarantee of forward bias. Coca-Cola is the perfect example. Historically a rock of predictability, Coca-Cola has experienced a shift in guidance bias. For most of its existence, it had no bias at all—it's guidance was near perfect. But over the past few years, Coca-Cola's guidance has on occasion wandered into the negative range.

When you're tracking guidance bias, keep Coca-Cola in mind. While I strongly believe that weighing bias is useful, it should be viewed as one tool in the arsenal, rather than as an absolute ax on valuation.

SUMMING UP

- What will ultimately happen in any given quarter is a mystery, but analysts try to predict earnings in advance. To help them along, companies provide guidance.

- Some companies consistently exceed expectations—they have a *positive* guidance bias. Some consistently miss expectations—they have a *negative* guidance bias.

- Because P/Es are partially based on consensus earnings estimates, and consensus earnings estimates are partially based on guidance, companies with a positive guidance bias often appear to be expensive, or overvalued.

- The best way to predict a company's earnings is to do so by quarter, not by year. Look at the revenue for each quarter over the past three years. Be alert to yearly trend lines and seasonal ones.

Quint Slattery was until recently the Manager of Pilgrim Baxter's $125 million New Opportunities Fund. As of March 31, 2000, his fund had a 12-month return of 533.05%, prompting *BusinessWeek* to say he was "in a league of his own" and *Fortune* to call him "the hottest new kid on the block." He is now a partner at Azure Capital Management, my new firm.

What was the best stock you ever owned? Why?

I began as a portfolio manager in mid-1998, at Pilgrim Baxter, just as the growth of Internet infrastructure was beginning to accelerate. Late 1997 and 1998 were the hallmark years of the dot-com era, and investors were bidding up stocks like crazy. What these investors failed to recognize was that companies selling regular goods over the Net had no defensible strategy to stop the commodization of their base businesses. Fortunately, I chose not to invest in the dot-com arena, for it seemed to me that while the Internet was revolutionary, the biggest growth opportunity lay in investing in companies that were establishing the *protocols* and *plumbing* for the Net.

I realized that the backbone that supported the Net was overwhelmed—I saw Internet transmission content (voice, data, and video) continuing to double every 90 days and video becoming more of a component on the Net. That's when I decided (in 1998) to focus my fund on companies that enhanced the creation of the Internet's infrastructure. I eventually funneled my fund down to cover 22 different subsectors of the Internet infrastructure, and they all contained compelling opportunities. It's difficult for me to pick one "best" company. But I guess from a stock return perspective, SDL Inc. performed the best for me.

What made you pick SDL Inc.?

It was late 1998, and I owned a company named JDS Uniphase. It was a company with an extremely compelling outlook in a fast-growing market (optics), but it had a history of spotty issues, particularly on the manufacturing side.

It was November 1998 when I bought SDL Inc. The overall stock market had been crushed in the previous month as the world worried about the Asian Crisis, a slowdown of global growth, and the demise of a once-highflying hedge fund called Long-Term Capital. JDS Uniphase and SDL Inc.

were both "arms merchants" in the emerging hypergrowth sector of optical networking. While JDS Uniphase was a pure play in this arena, SDL Inc. was not—it contained a slower-growth business unit that it was beginning to shed. Yet, both companies provided optical components and subsystems to an end market that had an insatiable desire and need for more goods, as the growth of the Internet continued.

By late 1999, optical networking was the largest explosive growth sector on Wall Street, with more than 12 companies up over 200 percent in stock price. By the end of the millennium, optics was the buzzword of Wall Street, as robust growth continued across the Internet and service providers poured major money into building out the infrastructure of the Net—an area in which SDL Inc., with its proprietary DWDM [dense wavelength-division multiplexing] products, dwelled almost alone. All the metrics continued to improve rapidly. In 1999 alone, SDL Inc. returned over 1,000 percent for me.

What is the number-one thing you look for in a company in which you're considering investing?

There are a few number-one things. I look for a ruthless management team; proprietary technology, preferably with some kind of intellectual property; accelerating long-term revenue growth; accelerating end-market growth; expanding margins; and pristine balance sheet metrics.

If you could give individual investors five minutes' worth of advice, what would it be?

Growth. Growth. Growth.

CHAPTER TWELVE

MIKE AND DANIELLE'S PORTFOLIOS

W e are now at the moment of truth, the moment when I will lay my investments at your feet—both good and bad—and explain my reasoning, or lack thereof. Some of my picks have done better than others. Luckily for me, the great ones have more than made up for the disasters. It's because of the great ones that my initial investment has grown 30 times over.

The poor picks, taken together, now make up less than 0.1 percent of my overall portfolio. Because they're so negligible, I have a strange habit—I refuse to sell them. I keep the disasters in my portfolio to remind me of flashes of extreme stupidity, so that anytime I'm tempted to go off half-cocked again, I will think twice.

In this book, I have tried to convince you that doing your homework is worth the effort. While you may get lucky now and then with a blind pick, if you want to earn 25 percent or more on your money, you have to put in the time. I know this to be true. Unfortunately, I have not always taken my own advice.

MIKE'S PORTFOLIO

I told you not to treat the stock market like a trip to Vegas. That advice is partly because of my own track record. In general, I've stuck to the rules laid out so far, but there have been a few times when I threw some money into the slots—betting on companies I knew next to nothing about. I bought stock in The Limited because a friend convinced me it was going to take over the teen clothing market. I bought stock in Canadian Southern Petroleum based on a tip from my broker.

I could go on, but I've got to retain *some* level of dignity. The point is, I bought these stocks for the wrong reasons. I trusted someone else's judgment, rather than making up my own mind. Even though some of them worked out pretty well, they were slot-machine investments. I had absolutely no knowledge of these companies, but I threw money into them, hoping they'd hit (see Figure 12.1).

FIGURE 12.1   MIKE'S PORTFOLIO AS OF DECEMBER 31, 1999.

COMPANY	PURCHASE DATE	PURCHASE PRICE*	VALUE
Applied Materials	April 1995	$14.00	$127.00
Boeing	August 1992	20.00	41.44
Cisco	November 1997	18.50	107.00
Compaq	January 1993	3.66	27.00
Dell	August 1992	0.30	51.00
Fannie Mae	January 1991	9.60	62.44
Ford	October 1993	18.50	53.31
Intel	August 1995	14.00	85.00
Microsoft	August 1989	0.75	117.00
PaineWebber	January 1996	13.00	39.00

*Adjusted for splits.
Note: These 10 stocks make up 99.9 percent of Mike's portfolio. Not listed are the 0.1 percent that Mike keeps around to remind him of his mistakes, as mentioned in the text.

As I mentioned in Chapter 1, while I believe five to seven stocks is the right amount for the average investor, I spend so much time immersed in the market that I've chosen to hold more. Let me state for the record that even with my experience, I'm not convinced that fattening my portfolio was a wise idea. Let me show you why.

99.9 percent of my stock pool is focused on 10 stocks. Seven of those stocks I know very well. The others I know less well. Of the seven I know very well, I've been averaging 25 percent per year or more on every single one. Of the stocks I know less well, I've managed 25 percent per year on only one. Learn from my mistakes (see Figure 12.2).

FIGURE 12.2   WELL-KNOWN AND UNKNOWN STOCKS IN MIKE'S PORTFOLIO.

Known Portion		
COMPANY	PURCHASE DATE	COMPOUND ANNUAL GAIN
Applied Materials	April 1995	60%
Cisco	November 1997	125
Compaq	January 1993	33
Dell	August 1992	101
Intel	August 1995	49
Microsoft	August 1989	63
PaineWebber	January 1996	32
Unknown Portion		
Boeing	August 1992	10%
Fannie Mae	January 1991	25
Ford	October 1993	19

Let's start with the known companies. What do I know very well? Well, I know high tech and I know the companies that I've worked for over the years.

Of the stocks that have done well in my portfolio, six are tech companies and one is a former employer, PaineWebber. Here's a quick roundup of what I bought, when I bought it, and why.

Cisco

When Internet stocks started going through the roof, lots of investors threw their money at start-ups. I chose to leave the upstarts and e-businesses alone and invest in the Internet by investing in the companies that supplied the infrastructure. One of those companies was Cisco.

Cisco supplies the products that route information through the Internet. I knew that if the Internet took off, Cisco's sales would, too. As the Internet's capacity increases, someone has to route the information.

I bought stock in 1997, when the investment community at large was sour on the company. It was cheap because of a minor problem that I knew the management would fix. I believed in the management, and I believed in the product. I did the math and realized that the stock was extremely undervalued. Public nervousness worked in my favor. I got a top company for bottom dollar.

Compaq

Summer 1992 brought the biggest change the PC industry had ever seen. As you may or may not recall from Chapter 6, that was when companies like Compaq and IBM started making the transition to building computers from standard parts.

At the time, I wasn't convinced that Compaq would be successful at making the switch. It had a bloated cost structure and had to either cut costs tremendously or quickly get its revenue up to cover them. While the company's business model was in flux, it was also attempting to reduce its gross margin to a pittance of what it had been before, in order to compete on price.

By early 1993, it was clear the company was getting somewhere.

In June 1992, a Compaq computer had cost customers 68 percent more than an equivalent Gateway machine. By early 1993, the difference was down to 20 percent. The cut in premium, combined with its superior brand name, put Compaq back in the game. Compaq also expanded distribution ferociously. Up until that point, both Compaq and IBM had limited who they allowed to sell their products. Now, at the height of IBM's dysfunction, Compaq made its products widely available at through scores of distributors. I suspected that Compaq would be able to steal some of IBM's market share while Big Blue was trying to get its act together. I bought in to Compaq.

The stock was a smart choice then, and it has remained so for most of the years since. But to be honest, I would have sold my shares in January 1998 if I had been allowed to do so. That was the month when I downgraded the stock for the first time in five years. Unfortunately, while the people who followed my coverage were able to bail out, I was not. I would have liked to have jumped ship, but industry rules prohibited me from doing so at that time.

INTEL

I bought Intel in 1995, in the midst of the PC gold rush, but at a time when the company itself was having some problems. Intel is the dominant player in computer processors. I thought the company had fantastic management, and besides that, it had a virtual stranglehold on the industry, providing chips for almost 90 percent of new computers.

That was then, this is now. Because of its dominant position, Intel has grown along with the PC industry. However, with the acceleration of PC sales beginning to slow, the stock could hit some trouble. Intel is attempting to branch out into other areas— networking, videotelephony, and application services. None have been all that successful as yet, but this doesn't mean they *won't* be.

In addition to these individual plays, Intel stands to make good money by riding in on another company's coattails. Microsoft, for example, is courting the high end of the server arena with Windows 2000, and should the product be successful, Intel's chips will move into the high-end server arena along with it. Hewlett-Packard has also committed to a relationship with Intel—HP is putting a new version of Unix on Intel's 64-bit processors.

With all these irons in the fire, Intel is likely to come out a winner. Going forward, I don't put the stock in the same class as Cisco, but I bought it cheap and I'm confident enough in the company to hold onto it and see how things play out.

PAINEWEBBER

I didn't exactly pick PaineWebber from scratch—I worked for the company and was given a certain number of shares along with my signing bonus. I did, however, choose to hang onto the stock long after I had left the company.

My reasoning was twofold. First, I knew the company well. I had observed management first-hand—after all, I worked there—and I agreed with the bulk of management's decisions. For example, I thought it was a smart move when the company expanded its retail brokerage side to give clients options like mutual funds, money management, and proprietary products. I felt that this expansion would keep clients from going somewhere else for these options. PaineWebber also had pretty good analysts (my colleagues) and a streamlined (if not so strong) investment banking side.

The second prong of my two-pronged positive analysis was this: PaineWebber, in my eyes, was ripe for acquisition. It was a smallish company, but a well-run one. In an age of consolidation, I was convinced that the company was a good target. Indeed, in the time I've held the stock, the company has come within a hair of being bought three or four times. I held onto the stock because I wasn't losing money on it, and because I'd make a killing if the company was ever bought. That day has yet to arrive; but who knows, it may. Then again, with retail brokerage houses facing increasing danger from Internet sites like e-Trade, I'll probably have liquidated this holding by the time this book hits the stores.

THE REST OF THE SUCCESSFUL SEVEN

My remaining three stocks are in Danielle's portfolio as well: Dell, Microsoft, and Applied Materials (see Figure 12.3). Dell and

FIGURE 12.3   DANIELLE'S PORTFOLIO AS OF
DECEMBER 31, 1999.

COMPANY	PURCHASE DATE	PURCHASE PRICE	VALUE	COMPOUND ANNUAL GAIN
Applied Materials	August 1995	$26.50	$126.70	43%
Dell	November 1997	9.00	51.00	123
Microsoft	June 1995	10.50	116.00	71

Microsoft are discussed at length elsewhere in the book, so I'm not going to go into our reasoning here. By now, it should be clear to you why I thought they were great investments.

Applied Materials makes products used in the manufacture of semiconductor chips. When a company like Intel makes a processor, it uses special equipment to do so. When Micron Technology makes memory chips, it needs special machinery. Applied Materials is the number-one supplier of that equipment.

One need only look at the direction in which the world is heading to know why Applied Materials is a good investment. As we move toward a world in which all information is converted into bytes (music, video, text, services, etc.), semiconductor sales will become even more rampant. The equipment Applied Materials provides will be needed to create semiconductors not only for PCs, but for everything else—phones, digital cameras, cars, electronics, and handheld devices.

The problem with investing in semiconductors themselves is the cyclical nature of the industry. The demand for equipment is much less volatile. When demand for chips is high, semiconductor companies need more equipment to make them. When demand is low, new equipment is still necessary, because the old equipment becomes obsolete as technology improves. You can't necessarily make a 64-bit chip with a 32-bit chip machine. The technology improves rapidly, regardless of whether the industry as a whole is growing. Because of this, I saw Applied Materials as a safe and interesting investment. I believed that it would outpace the semi-conductor area as a whole, and it has.

THE UNKNOWN PORTION
OF THE PORTFOLIO

Other than the truly blind investments mentioned early on in the chapter—the ones I keep around to remind me of my stupidity—I haven't dabbled all that much in nontech stocks. Thankfully, when I *have* dabbled, I have mainly done it with relatively small funds, but there are three exceptions: Boeing, the Federal National Mortgage Association (FNMA, known as Fannie Mae), and Ford.

BOEING

When I bought Boeing, it was a great philosophical thing to do. I'd been doing a tremendous amount of traveling for business, and at a certain juncture I realized that there were not enough planes. Plus, the planes in service were getting old, and with the number of people flying increasing exponentially, I thought that the airlines were going to have to replace their planes and add new ones. In retrospect, I turned out to be 100 percent right on that thinking.

Unfortunately, being right wasn't enough. My investment in Boeing is the perfect example of not spending enough time doing the analysis.

The problem with Boeing, in a word, was *management*. Boeing met the screen test. The valuation portion of the analysis was fine, and the company met this book's quantitative criteria, but I didn't pay attention to Boeing's track record. For the past 10 years, Boeing had completely mismanaged its opportunities. It continued to do so after I'd bought the stock.

Just as I'd anticipated, within the first few years that I owned the stock, orders for planes poured in to Boeing. The company was the number-one manufacturer of airplanes, with only one real competitor—Airbus, a European company. In fact, demand for Boeing planes was so high that orders were backlogged.

All of this should have been a boon for the company. Unfortunately, management did absolutely everything wrong. First, the company couldn't meet demand and manufacture enough planes. Then, management ran things so poorly that the planes the company *did* make weren't manufactured efficiently, so the profits weren't optimized. At another point, Boeing was plagued with employee strikes. Next, management lost a huge opportunity in Europe, by allowing Airbus to win virtually all the contracts on the continent. In short, the only thing Boeing did consistently was do almost everything wrong.

My investment in Boeing hasn't been a total disaster—I've doubled my money in the eight years I've owned the stock—but I wouldn't call it a victory. I've made 10 percent compounded return—more than I would have in a bank, but less than I would have made with a mutual fund. I've retained Boeing because the new management has committed to streamlining the cost structure and making other necessary changes. While I wouldn't recommend it to others, Boeing is a minimal part of my portfolio and it gives me some diversity beyond high tech.

FANNIE MAE

Unlike Boeing, Fannie Mae—formally the Federal National Mortgage Association (FNMA)—has been a pretty good investment. Mind you, it hasn't been a ringer, but I've made about 25 percent per year, which is lower than any of my tech stocks, but squeaks in above the target return. Fannie Mae is no superstar, but it's not unsatisfactory as a secondary holding.

I bought the stock primarily because I believed that it had a competitive advantage over other lenders. A friend had told me about its ties to the government and explained its history: Fannie Mae was created by Congress to bolster the housing industry during the Depression. Fannie Mae was originally part of the Federal Housing Administration, but became a private company operating with private capital in 1968. While it no longer officially received government backing, Fannie Mae still operated under a congressional charter. It had retained its position at the heart of the U.S. housing industry (a multi-trillion-dollar business sector) and it was the number-one provider of residential mortgages in America.

I soaked in his advice and then did some research on my own. I liked the fact that Fannie Mae worked with lenders, as opposed to working directly with homebuyers. I liked its focus—it dealt only with mortgages for low- to middle-income families. Most of all, I liked its track record—Fannie Mae was one of only seven companies in the S&P 500 that had produced double-digit increases in operating earnings for every one of the past 10 years. I decided to go for it.

Flash to nine years later. The stock has done pretty well by me. It's no 100-bagger, but it's closing in on a 7-bagger. Fannie Mae has turned in solid performance year after year. Of my nontech stocks, it's turned out to be one of the better ones.

FORD

I've owned two American-made cars in my lifetime. Neither one was a Ford. But while Ford's cars weren't particularly appealing to me, its stock was.

I bought stock in 1993, when Ford's valuation was ridiculously low. When I considered the stock's sticker price and looked at the management team the company had just brought in to turn things around, I felt that the stock was a steal. The Street was valuing Ford based on its past performance—or, should I say, underperformance. But Ford was in the process of a major overhaul, and I felt that it could turn things around.

As mentioned in the discussion of my beef with GM, American car companies failed to pay enough attention to quality control for much of the 1980s. Because of that, their market share dwindled. By the early 1990s, Ford recognized the problem and decided to change its manufacturing process to make its cars more competitive with their foreign counterparts. Ford also renegotiated deals with all the unions to improve its cost structure. Combining all this with the fact that the yen was steadily climbing against the dollar, Ford looked pretty good. With Japanese cars growing more and more expensive, I thought a well-made, well-priced American car could be competitive worldwide.

Ford's stock has tripled in the seven years I've owned it. It has also paid investors a dividend. (The current dividend is just under 4 percent, but in the past it was higher, and considering what I paid for the stock, any dividend at all is gravy to me.) All told, I've made over 20 percent a year on the car company. I could have made even more if I'd paid attention and sold a little sooner.

FIGURE 12.4   APPRECIATION ON MIKE'S PRIMARY INVESTMENTS AS OF DECEMBER 31, 1999, ASSUMING A $10,000 INVESTMENT IN EACH STOCK.

STOCK	ASSUMED INVESTMENT	APPRECIATION	VALUE
Tech Stocks			
Applied Materials	$10,000	9.1	$ 90,714
Cisco	10,000	5.8	57,838
Compaq	10,000	7.4	73,770
Dell	10,000	170.0	1,700,000
Intel	10,000	6.1	60,714
Microsoft	10,000	156.0	1,560,000
Subtotal	$60,000	59.1	$3,543,037
Nontech Stocks			
Boeing	$10,000	2.1	$ 20,720
Fannie Mae	10,000	6.5	65,042
Ford	10,000	2.9	28,811
PaineWebber	10,000	3.0	30,000
Subtotal	$40,000	3.6	$ 144,572

SUMMING UP

So there you have it: the good, the bad, and the ugly. As mentioned in Chapter 1, no one gets it all right. I am no exception; but despite my mistakes, I've made out like a bandit in my stock investments, and so has Danielle. Since 1995, her money has increased sixfold. Not bad for a formerly-starving artist.

As for me, my picks over the past 10 years, taken together, have had an average return of over 68 percent. What does this mean in cold, hard cash? Well, I'd rather not say exactly how much I have invested, but to give you an idea of how the percentages translate, let's say you had invested $10,000 in each one of the stocks in my portfolio at the time I bought them.

As of year-end 1999, you'd have more than tripled your money for the nontech portion. For the tech stocks, you'd have almost 60 times the original $60,000 (see Figure 12.4).

I'm not going to tell you how much I made. But it's safe to say that I'm not hurting, and my earnings are a direct result of the methods laid out in this book.

CHAPTER THIRTEEN

THE NEW TECHNOLOGY ERA

The 1990s was the age of the PC. Investors who got into companies like Dell, Microsoft, or Intel early saw their shares shoot up into the ether by the millennium New Year's Eve celebration.

Once PC stocks began to cool off a bit, many people started to view the Web as the next high-tech investment frontier. As a result, dozens of Internet start-ups saw their stock prices soar, mere minutes after they became public.

At this writing, the pendulum has swung the other way. By May 2000, the stock market, and tech stocks in particular, had hit bottom. The media trumpeted the end of an era. Many investors, especially day traders, panicked and liquidated their high-tech holdings. Even Alan Greenspan was kicking technology while it was down.

Without giving all the details of economic theory, let me point out that I believe the market had to come down. Some of the most coveted high-tech stocks were trading at irrationally high levels. The Federal Reserve Board had been raising interest rates to slow the market down, and that was bound to lead to lower stock prices eventually.

As of July 2000, tech stocks had yet to make a full recovery. However, on the bright side, for investors who've long been eyeing strong but overpriced companies, it's a great time to buy. While technology stocks are in the doghouse with the average investor, the technology industry is still rapidly increasing its share of the gross national product. The slump can't last for long.

A HIGH-TECH PRIMER

When I tell people that a market collapse is an ideal time to look into tech stocks, most of them head straight for e-commerce companies like Amazon, portals like Yahoo!, or internet service providers (ISPs) like America Online (AOL). While there's no question that many Internet companies hold promise as investments, Web plays like these are just the tip of the iceberg.

With more and more businesses going online every day, you could troll the e-commerce waters and attempt to pick a winner. But you should look deeper. Consider companies that supply the infrastructure that makes all of this e-commerce possible. Infrastructure will become extremely important as business after business faces the prospect of transforming itself to incorporate the Web.

There are hundreds of creative opportunities for those interested in investing in the future. Many of them are less known to the general public. This chapter discusses several key areas that have come about *because* of the Web, but are not necessarily typical Web investment plays. I'll point out some important, emerging areas that you should keep tabs on over the next few years.

LINUX

By the next millennium, the world may abandon the A.D. and B.C. designations altogether and refer to years as B.I. and A.I. (Before Internet and After Internet mass acceptance.) I'm only half joking. Perhaps no other invention has affected society quite so dramatically. Referring to things as B.I. and A.I. would draw a clear line as to when the Internet began to radically change the world.

Most people understand how the Web has changed the way we shop or changed the way we search for information. It has also rev-

1 0 SEGMENTS TO WATCH

1. Optics (e.g., LuxN and Calix)

2. Devices and intelligent appliances (e.g., Handspring and Research in Motion [RIM])

3. Open source and the companies surrounding it (e.g., VA Linux and Red Hat)

4. Application service providers (ASPs) and managed service providers (MSPs) (e.g., MimEcom and Aristasoft)

5. Wireless software infrastructure (e.g., Brience and ViAir)

6. Wireless device applications (e.g., Phone.com and AvantGo)

7. Fourth-wave business-to-consumer (B2C) companies that own content and access to consumers (e.g., Audible and Schwab)

8. Broadband (e.g., Broadcom and Jetstream)

9. Intelligent search engines (e.g., Ask Jeeves and HNC Software)

10. Commercial application providers (e.g., Art Technology Group and Vignette)

Note: Keep in mind that these companies are not purchase suggestions, they're intended as starting points for exploring each particular segment. At this writing, some of these companies have not gone public yet, but they may have by the time you read this.

olutionized some areas less known to the average Joe—things like product development. Linux is a perfect example, and it's an important area to watch as an investor.

Linux is a "new" operating system, based on one of the oldest operating systems around, Unix. It was created about nine years ago by Linus Torvalds, at that time a 21-year-old college student.

Let's take a step back in time. Before the Internet, operating systems were developed by a dedicated team working for one company (or one university) at one location, behind closed doors. Efforts at cooperation were often stymied, either by mistrust or because of geography.

Torvalds created the operating system equivalent of a commune. He put the ideas he had for Linux on the Web for all to see. He made it free for anyone who wanted to use it. He invited whoever had the skills and the inclination to participate in developing it. The only hitch? They wouldn't be paid for their work.

This online development cooperative was in fact quite radical. Many industry experts doubted that this "open source" model could work. How would Torvalds organize the project? Who in their right mind would volunteer?

Well, it turned out that many would. Torvalds was flooded with thousands and thousands of people eager to participate in his experiment.

How does it work? Every few months, two versions of Linux are released over the Web: a stable (production) product and a beta (test) version. Users can choose to download either one. Anyone using the beta version is encouraged to suggest improvements or identify bugs. Comments are then circulated over the Internet, and anyone with the inclination can attempt to code the enhancement or fix the bug. Once they send in their work, the enhancements and fixes are tested by other users. When the improvements are up to snuff, they're added to the next release. Once the beta version is viewed as being stable and complete, it becomes the next production version, and a new beta cycle begins.

The press has portrayed Linux developers as a group of wild-eyed radicals who want to change the world, but the developers drawn to the renegade nature of Linux make up only a small percent of all volunteers. Many of the people who work on Linux do it for good financial reasons. Companies that use Linux lend their employees; they want to influence what's brought onto the platform. Commercial companies that make money off of Linux also lend worker bees; these companies have a vested interest in the operating system's success.

Making money off of Linux? Wait a minute. Didn't I just tell you that Linux was free? Well, it is, sort of. The core version (or *kernel*) of the operating system is free. And Linus Torvalds himself doesn't make a penny off of Linux, but other people do. Like any other operating system, Linux needs utilities—applications that surround the kernel and make it more useful—such as a graphical user interface, server clustering, and directory services. Several companies (like Red Hat, Caldera Systems, SuSe, and TurboLinux) have popped up to distribute Linux and deliver utilities to surround the kernel.

Interestingly, just as the code for Linux is open source, so is the distribution. A customer can buy one copy from a company like Red Hat and then copy it as many times as he or she likes at no charge whatsoever. It's completely legal. With Linux, there is no such thing as pirating.

Hold on a minute, you're thinking, if Linux is free, why would anybody agree to pay for it in the first place? That's an interesting question. It turns out that companies like Red Hat are able to make a certain amount of money selling Linux in a box because the person who buys it from them (rather than downloading it off the Web for free) is entitled to services. Those who get it for free are on their own if something goes wrong. If you buy it in the box, you get a manual, documentation, and any technical support or handholding you need.

LINUX VERSUS MICROSOFT

Linux has grown like wildfire. It's especially popular with students, who love anything cheap and anything experimental. Linux is also the darling of academics and developers who believe that all software should be free and all source code should be readily available. Both the appeal of cooperative development and a belief that some balance is needed to tame the "Microsoft monster" have catapulted Linux into the spotlight as the most promising challenger to NT. A variety of the usual (anti-Microsoft) suspects have jumped on board to try to make this possibility a reality, including Oracle, IBM, Informix, Sybase, and Netscape.

It's unclear what Linux's future will hold. On one hand, the operating system has a lot going for it. Microsoft hasn't generated a high degree of faith, even among its friends. Its enemies have stoked the flames of mistrust, attempting to further undermine Microsoft's credibility. Plus, many people believe that Microsoft

INVESTING IN LINUX-BASED COMPANIES

Linux is a huge phenomenon, but it's a relatively new one. How much money a Linux-based company can make remains to be seen. It's clear that Linux hardware and services companies have a shot at something big. Investing in software distributors is a bit more risky.

Because Linux is available for free, companies that offer it in a box can charge only so much. Currently, only about 10 percent of the customers who choose Linux are willing to pay for it. If these companies tried to charge a price similar to what Microsoft charges for Windows or NT, the numbers would dwindle even further. On the flip side, a company like Red Hat or Caldera doesn't have to support the research and development budget of a company like Microsoft. Almost all the people working on the software are volunteers, so these companies have an edge economically.

As an investor, you need to weigh the pros and the cons for each of these Linux companies and see which, in your mind, wins out. You should also keep an eye out for new open-source entities, in the grand tradition of Linux, and the companies that emerge around them.

How open source will fare in the future, and who will rule the game if open source triumphs, is anybody's guess. This is a new model, and no one has the answers yet.

operating systems are less reliable than Linux. In a recent Datapro survey of more than 800 information systems managers and directors, Linux finished first in customer satisfaction, NT fifth.

Linux is free (or at least cheap). It's closely tied to Apache, a free open-source product that's the number-one Internet server. Linux is also the only high-end operating system besides NT to exhibit double-digit unit growth on the desktop.

However, while many people view Linux as a tremendous threat to Microsoft, I don't think Microsoft is in much danger. In fact, I think companies like Sun are more in jeopardy. At its core,

Linux is a derivative of the operating system Unix. The challenge to any company with a product based on Unix (like Sun, Compaq, IBM, and Hewlett-Packard) is to create a product that can run on any platform—a standardized version. If Linux could consolidate Unix, every single hardware vendor would be able to offer industry-standard Linux servers and desktops. The Unix market would start to gravitate toward the PC industry model, except that—unlike Windows—the operating system would be free.

This would place tremendous pressure on Unix hardware vendors like Sun, Hewlett-Packard, Compaq, and IBM, because customers would have the option of buying a more standardized computer, with the same robustness and scalability, for less money. Why would customers ever pay for a Unix operating system if they could get an equivalent one for free?

Far from losing out, Microsoft could actually *benefit* if Linux became more popular and displaced other Unix variants without eroding NT. Sun, on the other hand, would not.

Microsoft's losing to Linux may be a dream of many people in the industry, but it's a dream unlikely to come true. For Microsoft to be hurt, Linux would have to drive the Unix/Linux market share well beyond today's numbers. Then, and only then, would it become a significant long-term threat.

BETTING ON LINUX

You can't buy stock in Linux directly, but you can bet on the companies that surround it. If Linux is successful, these businesses are likely to benefit:

- Hardware vendors that use the Linux operating system for their servers or desktops
- Linux distributors
- Companies that provide maintenance or consulting services for Linux hardware and systems
- Vendors that create applications for Linux, such as general ledger, payroll, and so on

THE FUTURE

Whether Linux will win in the PC space remains to be seen, but it's already shaking things up. Dell has started to bundle the Linux operating system with some of its servers. I expect other vendors to follow suit. Linux desktop companies could win big with Linux because it helps their bottom lines. Microsoft charges a fee for every machine sold that runs Windows. Hardware vendors that fire their computers with Linux don't have to pay a red cent unless they want the technical support services that a Linux distributor like Red Hat can provide.

Linux is poised for success. Over the next few years, the operating system will go into everything from handhelds to appliances, set-top boxes to PCs. At this writing, it's too early to predict who the winners in the space will be, but there will be winners—big ones.

Some of those winners might not even be a blip on the Wall Street radar as yet. The platform is just too new. If you believe in Linux, follow industry developments. Then apply the rules in this book to any new companies that crop up.

SOLID, IF NOT SEXY

The following three areas may not be exciting investment areas, but they're important ones, and when it comes to high growth, they have high potential.

THE SAPs OF THE WEB

To be successful in the future, all companies are going to have to change the way that they do business. Every single corporation will have to integrate the Web into its business—from clothing catalogs to pizza parlors, from real estate agencies to washing machine companies.

Yesterday's Web sites were static. Customers visited primarily to search for information. There was little or no interaction between the site and the consumer. Tomorrow's Web sites will be "intelligent." A company's Web presence will be more than an online brochure or a rigid virtual storefront. Companies will seamlessly incorporate the Web and use what it has to offer.

Incorporating the Web doesn't have to be a drastic company transformation. It could be as simple as telling customers to go online to look for product information rather than including a manual with washing machines. Online troubleshooting is not only cheaper for the company to provide; it's faster and more convenient for the customer.

Were the company to go for broke, it might embed a chip in each washing machine that could be connected to the Web through a home network. The machine *itself* could send the customer an e-mail outlining the problem when it was time to schedule maintenance or replace a part. It could also automatically download do-it-yourself fix-it information or a list of local repair shops to the customer's computer. Futuristic? Maybe, but not far off.

In fact, early versions are already in place. Let's say, for example, you want to buy a car. Go to a live dealer and it's hard to get information on exactly how much certain options cost, which colors are available, what the reviewers have said, and so on. Dealers are too busy trying to sell you the car to dissect it for you.

Compare this experience to using a Web site like www.greenlight .com. Type in the model of car you're interested in, and a list of options pops up. Check off the ones you want, and the Web site prices your car accordingly. Have a question? Send an e-mail to a live person. When you've settled on the car of your dreams, punch in your contact information, and a service representative will check a number of different dealerships on your behalf, then call and tell you what's available. Greenlight is a prime example of *click and mortar:* a brick-and-mortar store that incorporates the best of the Web.

To be competitive in today's world, companies have to create Web sites that do more than advertise. They need Web sites that enhance their relationship with customers, Web sites that tailor content to the specific user sitting at the keyboard.

A number of entities have sprung up to help companies go from brick and mortar to click and mortar. They make Web applications—software that a company can personalize and use to integrate the Web with its existing business. These Web applications might help a company keep in touch with suppliers, track shipping, or balance its books. They might help a company put content online or keep track of its inventory.

In a nutshell, companies that make Web applications are the modern-day equivalent of companies like SAP and PeopleSoft. They've identified the needs of the average company and created standard applications to address those needs. SAP went from a tiny private company to a multi-billion-dollar business by creating core applications that every company required—software that handled general ledger, accounts payable, accounts receivable, and inventory services. Companies that make Web applications are trying to replicate SAP's success today and reap similar financial rewards.

What kinds of applications are they creating? Here's an example. Let's say you visit Amazon. Because of an application called WebLogic, you're able to get book recommendations based on what you've bought before. As you browse, the tool will also add things to your "shopping cart." When you click Order, it will validate your credit card, check that the book is in stock, figure out which warehouse has it, and decide how it will be shipped.

The appeal of Web applications is immediately evident: It would cost a fortune for most businesses to design a similar system in-house. The same holds true for most of the other applications being offered by specialists in the grand tradition of SAP.

Investors savvy enough to get into SAP early made a bundle. Companies that make Web applications hold the same potential. That's what makes this investment area one to watch.

At this writing, four of the biggest companies in the Web-application arena are Allaire, Vignette, Art Technology Group, and BroadVision, but lots of other companies play in this space. They offer everything from companywide meeting coordination to merchandise management.

One of my favorite applications is one created by a company called Blue Martini Software. It allows two friends in different cities to go shopping together via the Web. Each mouse click is communicated to the other browser, helping one friend lead the other through the online store. Similarly, a customer support representative could become an online personal shopper and help a customer find exactly what he or she is looking for.

OPTICS—SEE THE LIGHT

The Web is exploding. As more people and more businesses get onto the information superhighway, more lanes are needed to deal with the traffic.

These lanes are increasingly made of optical fiber. In 1999 alone, 65 million kilometers of fiber was installed in the United States. Basically, optical fiber is very big pipe for transmitting data, as opposed to electronically oriented copper and coaxial cable. Information is shot through the pipe by laser, on a beam of light.

Because of the ever-expanding need for fast and high-bandwidth Internet delivery, the optical networking industry is growing by leaps and bounds. Telecommunications carriers are rushing to upgrade their infrastructures to keep pace with demand. Experts predict that optics will affect the telecommunications industry in much the same way that the personal computer affected the computing industry 20 years ago. In other words, it's going to be huge.

How huge? Well there's already more than $200 billion worth of voice-centric equipment in place, but it's overtaxed, outdated, and in need of major overhaul. This overhaul alone will bring huge revenues to the optical networking industry, but in addition to updating equipment and laying enough high-speed fiber to pass massive streams of information, there's a need for making that information pass through the network as efficiently as possible. (Companies like Lucent, Ciena, Nortel Networks, Sycamore Networks, and Corvis make this work.)

Let's say you're in Atlanta, sending data to Oregon. Optical fiber is in place to make this happen, but your data isn't sent in a straight line. Instead, it is passed through several hubs along the way. Companies such as Cyras Systems, ONI Systems, Nortel

(Continued)

Networks, and Zaffire transport and direct information to regional network environments and hubs. Then there are companies (like JDS Uniphase, SDL, and AMCC) that supply the optical tools and components to build the equipment itself.

In the not-so-distant future, optical networking will extend directly into offices and neighborhoods. Systems companies like LuxN and World Wide Packets are positioning themselves to get ready for that eventuality.

One day, after costs have come down out of the stratosphere, you may be able to attach your PC to an optical link from home and get information at the speed of light. Until then, you can at least own the stocks.

APPLICATION SERVICE PROVIDERS

Web applications cut out a lot of the work for companies, because there's no need to design tools from scratch, but companies still require equipment. Some companies just don't have the room, or the funds up front, for that equipment. This is where the application service provider (ASP) comes into the picture. ASPs offer off-site data centers that host specific applications.

The idea isn't a new one, although the technology may be. I remember that years ago, when I ran a computer software and consulting company, we used to dial into a remote service provider. It was called *time-sharing* in those days. You actually dialed in to the computers by telephone. Prehistoric, I know. Time-sharing had its place, but it was very expensive and very limited: Companies had to put in direct lines running from every location.

The Web has created a cheap and far more efficient system. If you think about it, what is the Web, but a tremendous communication infrastructure? Because of this new information superhighway, a company can now set up a remote service provider anywhere in the world and its customers, or sales representatives, or whomever, can connect to it from wherever they are, through the Web.

These remote data centers can run any number of applications, from e-commerce to computer aided design. In the early

WHERE HAS ALL THE TALENT GONE?

You're a systems engineer. You've just graduated from college. You get two job offers that pay the same amount. One company specializes in systems. The other specializes in shoes. Both need their systems kept up and running. Which do you choose?

Well, obviously, as a systems engineer, the systems company seems more attractive. And that's why shoe companies trying to go click-and-mortar are going to have a hard time hiring tech workers. In fact, that's why almost every company is going to have trouble.

If you read the papers, you'll know that our country is facing a huge crisis in terms of recruiting information technology (IT) specialists. It's only going to get worse. The U.S. Department of Labor estimates that today's 400,000 shortfall of high-tech staff will grow to 4 million by 2002.

Because experienced IT professionals are growing scarcer by the second, it's becoming ever more likely that these professionals will be centralized. Economically, it makes more sense to have these people serve a whole bunch of companies, rather than expect the scant resources of most small businesses to be enough to recruit them to work in-house.

Managed service providers (MSPs) are springing up to fill this need. They keep technical equipment in working order for a set of companies from a centralized location. Usually, they install monitoring systems on the company's computers—or the computers the companys have in effect leased through an ASP—and keep an eye on things from afar. Should a problem arise, they can usually fix it by examining the information sent via these extremely expensive monitoring systems.

The efficiency and expertise brought about by MSPs makes them a force to be reckoned with. They are certainly an area to watch for the new millennium.

days of the Web they were hosts, nothing more. ASPs take this idea one step further: They offer the hosting and the application itself.

Here's an example: ThinkLink is an ASP that specializes in communications. It's meant to deal with one of my primary pet peeves—too many messages.

As far as I'm concerned, one of the major inconveniences of the modern era is that there are too many ways for people to contact you. Voicemail, e-mail, faxes, instant messaging, cell phone, home phone—the list goes on. ThinkLink offers integrated messaging for businesses. Employees can access all their messages from one location, either by phone or online, no matter where they happen to be. The application makes it possible, through text-to-speech technology, to have faxes and e-mails read aloud over the phone. Likewise, the technology is able to translate voice messages into text. It allows for paging, message alert, forwarding, and message transfer. If you'd like, you can even program the system to find you at all times (though why anyone in their right mind would do this, I have no idea).

Experts predict that by 2002, Americans alone will leave 1.5 billion e-mail messages. With instant access becoming an ever-more-prevalent expectation, a system capable of sorting and facilitating communication will be valuable to almost any small business.

An ASP is an attractive option for companies that want to take care of in-house infrastructure shortfalls in a quick and easy way. However, ASPs do more than make things easier—they usually make things cheaper.

To get a handle on why the financials work in their favor, consider Automatic Data Processing (ADP), the payroll company. In a way, ADP is an old-world version of the ASP model. Because ADP specializes in payroll, and payroll only, it has better economics than a company trying to do everything (including payroll) itself. Because of economies of scale, ADP can do payroll better, quicker, and for less money and still make a profit. For similar reasons, so can ASPs.

SET-TOP BOXES

Businesses will be completely transformed by the Web, and so will home life. The Web has wormed its way into the daily lives of a huge chunk of the general population, but it will penetrate even further.

One of the major ways that the Web will go home is through television set-top boxes.

Yesterday's Box

The set-top box is hardly fresh-faced. It was first touted as the next new thing in September 1993, when Time Warner put out a white paper titled "The Full Service Network." The paper trumpeted the coming cable revolution and predicted a wide rollout of digital set-top-box subscribers by 1998.

At about the same time, Microsoft demonstrated its vision of interactive television and associated e-commerce at an analysts meeting I attended. These factors helped drive up cable and set-top-box stocks an average of 76 percent in 1993.

The problem was that the excitement was too early. Memory was expensive, routing capability was insufficient, bandwidth was limited, and compression technology was in its infancy.

People had big dreams for the set-top box in 1993, but the technology wasn't there to make them a reality. They imagined a vast movie library at the click of a button, shot right to your television, with fast-forwarding and rewinding features. But for video on demand to offer the features of a VCR, plus the same variety of movies available at a rental store, much memory and disk capacity were needed.

In 1993, server memory (DRAM) cost a whopping $25 per megabyte. Putting a mere 20 minutes of a movie in memory would have required roughly $30,000 worth of DRAM (see Figure 13.1). Add this problem to the ridiculous disk requirements and a host of other issues, and the cost per cable subscriber for the services envisioned in the white paper would have been in the $10,000 range. And you thought *your* cable bill was high.

Today's Box

That was then, this is now. Since 1995, three major things have taken place: (1) the Internet has been accepted by the mass market; (2) cable infrastructure, set-top-box, and server costs have come down; and (3) digital television sets have started to appear.

Mass adoption of the Internet means that for the first time,

FIGURE 13.1   APPROXIMATE COST PER MOVIE IN USE.

FACTOR	1993	1999
Megabytes/frame*	1	1
Frames/second	30	30
Actual compression*	$\frac{1}{30}$	$\frac{1}{150}$
Seconds/minute	60	60
Megabytes/minute	60.0	12.0
$/megabyte	25.00	1.08
Minutes/movie	20	20
Cost/movie	$30,000	$259

*Rounded figures.

there's a good *reason* for digital set-top boxes—providing high-bandwidth Internet access. Reductions in cost mean that delivering this kind of service isn't financially masochistic. Also, with services *beyond* bandwidth delivery—such as Internet telephony, chat, messaging, electronic program guides, mail, digital music downloading, and others—companies that deliver bandwidth through set-top boxes can offer even more and earn more because of it. The kicker is that the cost of bundled cable service will be less expensive to the consumer than buying things à la carte (for example, basic cable, an ISP, and an extra phone line for the home modem; see Figure 13.2). By 2005, I expect about 78 million people to have access to a high-bandwidth pipeline from their homes, mostly through cable and DSL. By then, digital television may also start taking hold. As we enter the new decade, the set-top box is becoming an engaging reality.

Tomorrow's Box

Companies such as WebTV have been offering versions of the set-top box for several years now. Unfortunately, those early versions

FIGURE 13.2   COMPARISON OF COST OF SERVICES—
BUNDLED VERSUS SEPARATE
PURCHASES

SERVICE	COST
Basic cable	$25
ISP	20
Phone line connecting ISP	20
Voice phone line	20
Total	$85
Cable service bundled with ISP and other features	$50–$60

were pretty uninspiring—they did little more than let you check your e-mail or *very* slowly search the Web.

Well, say goodbye to yesteryear. Tomorrow's set-top box will do much more. Flying through your cable wires and coming at you through something that looks similar to today's cable box, the new set-top box will be able to interact both with your cable programming and with normal network television.

What do I mean by *interact*? In the very near future, a piece of each and every television broadcast will be set aside for data shot to the set-top box. The extra information might be content that broadens a viewer's knowledge. It might be something that stimulates interactive dialog. It might be commerce associated with the show being viewed. Whatever form it takes, viewers will be able to interact with their televisions and not only receive information, but send information back.

Let's say you're watching a game show like *Who Wants to Be a Millionaire*. Instead of merely shouting answers at your television set, you could shrink the show to a small box on your screen and then play the game live, in real time, as it goes along. Your answers would be broadcast back through your television. The network would receive the answers, and the highest-scoring people playing at home might be brought in to play the game with Regis for real.

Here's another example. Let's say you live in San Francisco. You could care less about weather in Poughkeepsie, or even, for that matter, Sacramento. With this new technology, the Weather Channel will be able to detect your exact location from your data signal and then give you the weather that applies to you—Not just for your city, for your *block*.

Networks might poll viewers on public issues or ask them what they think of a new show, and the results could have a direct impact on future content. The Emmy Awards broadcast, several game shows, and *Sesame Street* are already using this kind of technology.

Once commerce becomes part of the picture, things get really interesting. When the 10 o'clock news show does a feature on a musician or discusses a sports team, it could offer sales of concert or game tickets. When an actor's outfit catches your eye while you're watching your favorite sitcom, you could click on it and buy the pants or shirt immediately. The same goes for background music, related books, and travel information surrounding a location shot. Televisions connected to a set-top box could also be used for Internet telephony. Because of the broadband capability provided through the cable company, they could potentially be used for video phone calls as well.

Set-top boxes will allow you to download music and movies with ease. They'll also make television watching much more pleasurable—get up for a snack or to answer the phone, hit a button, and the box will start recording your show digitally. When you come back, it will pick up where you left off.

The set-top box is likely to come into high-volume use—I wouldn't be surprised to see 25 to 50 million digital boxes in place by 2005. At this writing, the big players in the set-top space are companies such as Liberate, Microsoft, Open TV, and France's Canal Plus (software companies that provide the platform that makes it all work); MetaTV (which makes applications that sit on top of this software); Gemstar (which offers an electronic TV guide); Scientific Atlanta and General Instrument (which manufacture the boxes themselves); cable, satellite, and DSL companies (which provide access to the connection); and broadband providers (which physically lay the fiber).

Of course, within a year, the key players may have changed, but keeping track of who provides the infrastructure to make set-top boxes and broadband possible will stand you in good stead to make a judgment call on individual stocks. Companies that manufacture the fiber, own the fiber, and produce materials for the fiber also have big potential in the coming years, as do companies that provide the modems, chips, and other components that make broadband connections possible.

SUMMING UP

There are many Internet investment opportunities beyond e-commerce. It's too soon to tell which technologies will win out, but it's not too soon to start tracking them. Focus on companies that provide the infrastructure that make the Web possible, such as the following:

- Linux-based companies
- Web application providers that help traditional businesses merge the Web with their existing infrastructure
- Application service providers—off-site data centers that host business applications
- Set-top-box facilitators—the companies surrounding and supporting these cable-installed home portals
- Infrastructure providers in areas like optics, software, and broadband—companies that will help create the capacity necessary for the expansion of the Internet

CHAPTER FOURTEEN

THE FOURTH WAVE OF THE WEB

A mere 25 years ago, few people predicted that by 2000 there would be a computer in well over half the homes in America. Fifteen years ago, no one thought we'd all be carrying cell phones. Ten years ago, no one could have imagined we'd enter the new century with more than half the world online. Technology has brought about many changes, but the fourth wave of the Web, a huge phenomenon about to strike, stands to be the greatest societal transformation we have ever seen.

HISTORY LESSON

To understand the fourth wave of the Web, you need to understand the three waves that came before it. Let me take you back to the early 1970s. Disco was king, bell bottoms were still acceptable, and the first seeds of what would become the Internet were being planted.

THE FIRST WAVE: COMMUNICATIONS

E-mail may seem like a newfangled phenomenon, but believe it or not, the first e-mail program was invented in 1971. It was used over a distributed network within an organization, so while it was Internet connected, it wasn't really Internet based. By the mid-1970s, e-mail communication began to spread its wings and become rampant among researchers and academics. By the early 1990s, lots of corporations had followed suit—AT&T Mail, MCI Mail, Lotus Mail, and others.

THE SECOND WAVE: CONTENT

In 1990, the world at large started to come online. Before that, access to the Internet had been almost exclusively restricted to academia, government agencies, and research organizations. Users had to be part of one of these large entities in order to gain online access. 1990 brought a monumental announcement from the World Standard company (world.std.com): Dial-up access would be available to anyone willing to pay for it. With a commercial provider of Internet access now on the scene, individuals could connect to the Internet from their homes for the first time in history.

As important as all of these developments were, the release of Netscape Navigator on August 9, 1995, was the real breakthrough. Navigator was the first retail browser, and it revolutionized the online experience. No sooner had Netscape released the product than Microsoft responded by distributing its own browser, Internet Explorer, for free. Suddenly, the Internet shed its unwieldiness and Web usage exploded. Even investors started taking notice of the Internet's potential, and Netscape was their poster child.

With the advent of the World Wide Web, the second wave flowed beyond academia. A new generation of sites cropped up, placing information at thousands of fingertips. Yahoo!, America Online (AOL), and a handful of other providers made personalizing content delivery an art form, in the hopes of expanding the time spent on their respective portals. The second wave was somewhat akin to the television model; each portal was like a network with advertising the primary goal, and internet service providers (ISPs) were like the cable operators.

THE THIRD WAVE: E-COMMERCE

Once many people were connected to the Web, it started making sense to sell things there. Amazon was one of the true trailblazers in e-commerce. It began selling books online in 1996, completely ignoring the brick-and-mortar model and forging a new path for online commerce.

Companies like eToys, eBay, Dell, Buy.com, and others soon followed. E-commerce was a new frontier, and each of these companies created its own method of selling directly to the customer through the Web. Some sites were more successful than others, but all seemed to capture investors' imagination.

Traditional e-commerce was a boon for the customer because it offered lower prices and better access to product information. Unfortunately, it didn't give the vendor a very big cost advantage.

Consider Amazon for a moment. "The world's largest bookstore" offers a tremendous service to customers. Customers have access to tens of thousands of products from the comfort of their homes; they're given targeted suggestions for products based on what they've bought from Amazon in the past; and they have access to excerpts and reviews. As wonderful as all of this is for the customer, it's not a huge economic breakthrough for Amazon. The company has a convenience edge over Barnes & Noble, Borders, or any other brick-and-mortar store, but it's still doing business the traditional way.

The problem with the third wave of the Web is that it still involves physical delivery. When a customer orders a book from Amazon, or a CD from CDNOW, or a Palm Pilot from Buy.com, these companies have to go to their warehouses, pick the order, wrap it up, and arrange for it to be delivered by UPS or some other carrier. Although the companies use the Internet to court their customers, these vendors are still storing and shipping a physical product.

THE FOURTH WAVE: REPLACEMENT OF PHYSICAL PRODUCT

With the fourth wave of the Web, warehouses, storage, and shipping are a thing of the past. In many instances, it will also completely eliminate the need for manufacturing, inventory, tracking, shipping, returns processing, and other key current company expenses. When the wave hits, commodities will be shipped in bytes, not boxes.

Investors interested in high-tech stocks need to understand the fourth wave; it will provide a foothold for many new companies to squeeze their way into the marketplace and reap huge financial rewards. It will also put the stalwarts of many industries at great risk, should they be slow to transform themselves.

The fourth wave consists of two major categories of products: physical and service. By *physical,* I mean products that are *currently* physical. This first category covers products that are, at present, being manufactured, but ones that have the potential to be stored digitally and then shipped in bytes. Once they reach the customer, they'll be brought back to life by a computer or some other device. Music, books, spoken audio, video, photographs—all of these things fall under the physical category.

By *service* products, I mean things like brokerage, insurance, mortgage lending, training, and customer support. In each of these cases, the fourth wave will eliminate the need to have *people* provide the service. It will be provided, through the Internet, by each customer's computer.

If you've ever tried to get a technical question answered through a customer support line and ended up in voicemail hell, you're probably not too anxious to consider computer-generated service products. But truth be told, if computer support is done right, it will give better results more consistently than all but a handful of individuals.

Think of the best computer chess games. Programmed correctly, the games use strategies that would be deployed by a world-class player. A computer can beat virtually any chess player in the world, because no matter how good a person is, no human can store every possibility in his or her brain at all times.

Like a computerized chess game, the premiere fourth-wave support products will take the best features and practices from a set of humans—whether in the fields of suggesting stocks, recommending loans, finding insurance, or matching mortgages—and program them into the computer so they'll benefit every customer, every time. As much as you might hate to admit it, it's very hard for an individual to match that. Only a small number of individuals on this planet could do so.

With fourth-wave service products, companies will be able to (1) deliver a service in bytes that's actually as good or better than what's delivered by people, (2) eliminate all the cost of employing the people, and (3) send it right to customers' homes, to be accessed at their convenience, with no waiting time.

This is a model that's hard to beat. Why do you think that more than half of Dell's customer support is now supplied via the Web? Not only are Dell's customers happier with the level of service and convenience they get with Web support, the cost to Dell has shrunk from about $50 per incident to close to zero.

Another fourth-wave service that's come on fast is online brokerage. In 1997, only about 7 percent of all retail trading was done online. A year later, it was closer to 11 percent. In the first quarter of 1999, it was 16 percent. I'm guessing that by the end of 2000 it will approach 30 percent.

The fourth wave is transforming the brokerage industry. Customers can now peruse stocks at their leisure, 24 hours a day, 7 days a week, just by sitting down at the computer. They have access to industry research and real-time stock quotes, plus the ability to make trades for $10 to $20 a hit, rather than hundreds of dollars.

This plethora of privileges costs the service provider pennies per person, and it's shaken the industry to its core. In order to compete, brick-and-mortar brokerage houses have to offer customers more than what is available online. They have to give customers a level of service and attention unlike anything these institutions have ever had to provide before.

SUBSTANTIAL COMPETITIVE ADVANTAGES CREATED BY THE FOURTH WAVE

Let's get back to Amazon. As mentioned, Amazon's model has taken much of the cost out of selling a product, but it represents only a small piece of the Web's potential. Right now, when an e-commerce company like Amazon takes an order, fulfillment looks similar to a traditional mail-order model. With the coming of the fourth wave, books will eventually be downloaded off the Internet, rather than shipped from a warehouse. The customer will pay less, but both the publisher and the author will make more money, because the cost of producing a book will be greatly reduced: There will be no need for paper, absolutely no printing costs, no binding, no remainders, no UPS tracking, and no processing of returns (see Figure 14.1).

FIGURE 14.1 TRADITIONAL VERSUS ELECTRONIC PUBLISHING.

	METHOD		
FACTOR	**TRADITIONAL**	**ELECTRONIC**	**CHANGE**
Production cost*	$4.08	$0.00	−100%
Creation cost			
Editing	0.45	0.45	0
Royalties	1.45	1.45	0
Marketing and advertising	1.25	1.25	0
Sales commission (8%)[†]	0.80	0.48	−40
Total publishing cost	$8.03	$3.63	−55%
Gross profit to publisher	$1.97	$2.37	20%
Cost to distributor	$10.00	$6.00	−40%
Gross profit to distributor	$4.00	$4.00	0%
Price to end consumer[‡]	$14.00	$10.00	−29%

*Includes $3.25 for paper, printing, and binding; $0.30 for bulk shipping; and $0.53 allocation cost for returns.
[†]Calculated on distributor's cost.
[‡]$20 list price with 30 percent discount and no discount for electronically distributed books.

Big Things in Small Packages

Amazon has an advertisement that shows the Taj Mahal and says something like, "We have so much inventory, we could fill the Taj Mahal." Impressive, and yet, problematic. With that much stock, you *need* a Taj Mahal. Think of the cost of all that warehousing and inventory.

If Amazon had all of its products stored in bytes, not boxes, all it would need would be a few disk drives to store the same inventory. A disk drive doesn't take up much room—the company could commandeer a little *corner* of the Taj Mahal, even a closet, and house the disk drives needed to store every book ever made.

In music, transforming products from physical to digital is even easier than it is in publishing. CDs are digitally recorded, so the music is actually already stored in bytes.

With the fourth wave, there will be no such thing as a hard-to-find recording. People will be able to purchase any album that exists in the world with a few keystrokes.

How will it work? Let's say you're a Beatles fan. You'd go to your favorite site, where they'd already know who you are and have a record of how you like to pay. You'd type in *Rubber Soul,* hit Order, and the music would be automatically and instantaneously downloaded to your computer's hard drive, or some other device with the memory to store it (such as a Rio or Sony's Music Clip). Talk about immediate gratification!

The fourth wave is a godsend for consumers, but it's a dream for companies as well. Compared to traditional means, products will cost next to nothing to produce. Take audio books. To get an audio book to market, a traditional producer has to record the book, manufacture it (by putting it on a cassette tape), package it, and ship it to hundreds, maybe even thousands, of brick-and-mortar storefronts. All of this translates into a variable cost of about $12 per audio book.

In contrast, a company like Audible, which delivers the same content directly to the customer in bytes, can shoot the same book down the online superhighway for pennies (see Figure 14.2). The price discrepancy isn't lost on Amazon. The company recently signed a deal with Audible to deliver spoken audio content

FIGURE 14.2   TRADITIONAL SPOKEN AUDIO COST
VERSUS DIGITAL PUBLISHING.

	METHOD		
FACTOR	TRADITIONAL	DIGITAL	CHANGE
Manufacturing and packaging	$ 3.00	$0.00	−100%
Inventory	0.50	0.00	−100
Shipping, handling, and returns	2.50	0.00	−100
Retailer cost	6.00	0.00	−100
Total	$12.00	$0.00	−100%

Note: Table compares only costs that differ. Both methods have royalties, recording cost, creation cost, and so on.

through its site—everything from best sellers to newspapers, from a comedy show hosted by Robin Williams to a selection of National Public Radio programs.

Once a traditional producer factors in the cost of marketing, manufacturing, distribution, and all other costs, the potential profit on physical items is a few dollars, maximum. In the music industry, for example, a label makes about $5.30 in profits on a CD priced at $17.99. (The artist typically gets $1 or less.)

With the fourth wave, a company that ships that same album in bytes could make $10.84 in profits. And that's assuming the label more than triples the amount paid to the artist. In actuality, what a label does with the extra profit is up to it. The label could share more with the artist, give a discount to the customer, or keep the money itself (see Figure 14.3). Whatever it decides to do, it has a bigger margin to play with.

THE FOURTH WAVE AND YOU

So far, I've focused mainly on the commercial element of the fourth wave, but while it's true that it will affect the way you shop, it

FIGURE 14.3   FOURTH WAVE VERSUS BRICK
AND MORTAR—MUSIC.

	METHOD	
FACTOR	TRADITIONAL	DIGITAL
Marketing	$ 0.75	$ 0.75
Manufacturing	1.10	0.10
Distribution	2.30	0.10
Mechanical royalties	0.70	0.70
Retailer	6.59	1.50
Average artist royalty	1.25	4.00
Label profit or discount	5.30	10.84
Subtotal	$17.99	$17.99

LEFT TO YOUR OWN DEVICES

The fourth wave is racing toward us. In some arenas, it is already becoming a reality. However, in order for the fourth wave to reach its full potential, several key enablers are needed:

- *Greater bandwidth,* so delivery is fast
- *Appropriate devices,* so customers can take content on the road
- *Increased security,* so artists and authors know they're being paid for every product sold
- *Reasonable price points,* to encourage customers to make the switch
- *Ease of use,* so content is a snap to download, transmit, and play immediately

will affect the way you live even more. The fourth wave will shake up e-commerce, but it will also shake up your e-mail correspondence, your drive to work—even your photo album. As more and more people jump on the wave, individuals are likely to want to exchange fourth-wave products.

We're already in the early stages. I witnessed the fourth wave a few months ago when I hooked into my e-mail. Danielle had recently gotten married, and some of her friends had taken pictures of the wedding with digital cameras. Once they were home, they loaded them onto the computer, posted them onto a Web site, and e-mailed the Web address to everyone they'd met at the party. Guests like me could download pictures off the site, put photographic paper into their printers, and get pictures immediately.

Sony has just introduced a "digital picture frame" that will make even printouts passé. The digital frame can display photos stored on the PC or taken from the Web, and it can change the picture automatically, as frequently as you wish.

As I said, these are the early stages. Soon, people won't carry regular pictures in their wallets. Instead, everyone will carry a handheld device. People will be able to download pictures with perfect resolution, in color, and if they want to exchange them with Grandma, they'll be able to beam the pictures from one handheld to another. Business cards, videos, newsletters, books, statistics, Web sites, and more will be passed digitally, not sent by mail or exchanged by hand.

Handheld devices offer compelling possibilities, but I don't foresee them replacing home computers. Instead, I think people will download music or books onto a computer and then beam them onto a portable device. I'm betting that most people will still want to do word processing on a desktop, but they'll use devices to listen to music while taking a jog, or they'll beam *Hamlet* onto an e-book for a little light reading.

You may think that you'll never give up your dog-eared hardcovers and throw an e-book into your briefcase, but believe me, you will. I, too, was a naysayer. On a recent trip to Hawaii, I agreed to take the e-book, just to test it out. First of all, I'm a huge reader, so the first thing I noticed was that my luggage was about 10 pounds lighter. I'd expected that. What I didn't expect was the resolution of the screen. It was actually *easier* to read than many printed books. While no self-respecting book requires a battery, this high-tech version had a weight similar to that of its traditional counterpart—but it held about 10 novels.

Other perks? My wife and I could have more than one novel open at a time. We could bookmark where we'd left off. We could even look up words we didn't know. The e-book may not be quite as comfy as the paper version, but it's well on its way to becoming a real alternative.

THE FUTURE OF THE FOURTH WAVE

This is the direction in which I see society going: People will store libraries of music, books, photos, movies, and other things on their PCs and then download them into appropriate devices so they can take the content on the road. They'll use e-books for reading, set-top boxes to view interactive content through their televisions, MP3 players (like the Rio) for music, and audio players for downloading newspapers, comics, spoken audio, games, and other things. Or, they'll have devices that handle several types of content at once. They'll have smart phones that, at minimum, let them surf the Web and handheld devices to input business cards, get stock quotes, check and respond to e-mail, or scan small images.

Imagine this: You have an audio version of the *Wall Street Journal* automatically downloaded from your computer each night to the handheld device you have connected to your PC through a cradle. Or, through a wireless network, you beam the newspaper to a device in your car and listen to the *Journal* from your Auto PC on your way to work. Better yet, unlike the printed version, the digital version will be customized. The stock quotes that greet you each morning during your daily commute will be stocks you own. Articles will be automatically screened to match your taste, and they'll play in order of what you'd probably like to hear first. Sound futuristic? Well, we're not quite there yet, but believe it or not, most of the elements to make this possible are already in place. Many of the luxury cars that ship for the 2002 model year will have Auto PCs, voice-activated computers that let you do everything from call your mom to figure out when you should change lanes and get off the highway, all hands-free.

SAFE OR SORRY?

For the fourth wave to really take off, developers need to put security first. In 1999 alone, American firms lost over $12 billion to piracy. Book publishers, record companies, and movie studios fear that making their products available in digital format through the Web will make piracy more rampant and that it will be even more difficult to protect their intellectual property.

Security in the computer industry is hardly a new problem. Software companies have dealt with piracy from the onset. In the early 1990s, about three copies of software were pirated for every one sold. After years of diligent effort, that number has been cut almost in half.

MP3, a popular format for storing music, makes it easy to send downloaded songs to friends or to distribute them illegally. The Recording Industry Association of America (RIAA) initially reacted to this by suing Diamond Multimedia, the company that produced the Rio (acquired in September 1999 by S3 Inc.). Had Diamond continued to market the Rio as a playback device, it probably would not have lost the case, but because it ventured into hosting customers' music libraries on its site, it got into trouble. Hosting a customer's music library and allowing others to get at it was seen by the courts as a copyright violation.

The suit was a nightmare for Diamond Multimedia, but it was a turning point for online music. It spurred the high-tech industry to take RIAA seriously and start to explore improved methods of security.

While I understand the fear that surrounds digital music, I think it's unwarranted. In fact, I believe that the fourth wave, done right, will actually *reduce* music piracy. Since the late 1990's, many consumers have been putting CD content onto their computers through a CD-ROM drive and sending the music to all of their friends as e-mail attachments. Other people routinely burn copies of their favorite CDs onto blank disks and give them away. Downloading music may scare record companies silly, but in reality, CDs are far less secure than the digital formats of the future are likely to be.

Fear of piracy and fear of lawsuits have prompted many fourth-wave companies to introduce safeguards. Nuvo Media (maker of the Rocket eBook) and Audible (broker of spoken audio content) enforce copyright protection through encryption technology. It works by ensuring that the device owned by the person who purchased the title is the only device able to decrypt the purchased text. Similar solutions are under development for maps, video, photos, and other content.

CATCHING THE WAVE

Other than safety, the key components of the fourth wave will be portals (like AOL and Yahoo!) that integrate video and data to provide broadband content (television and other things broadcast through the Web), software companies (like Liberate and BSQUARE) that empower set-top boxes and handheld devices, the handheld device companies themselves (like Palm, Handspring, and companies developing devices for Windows CE), and broadband enablers (like cable and DSL providers).

Some of the stalwarts from the pretechnology generation could be important, too. For example Clarion, the stereo company, is developing Auto PCs. Hewlett-Packard is producing low-cost printers that can print very high quality photographs. Kodak is offering digital camera attachments to Palm and Handspring devices and has struck an agreement with Hewlett-Packard to transmit digital pictures directly from cameras to HP photographic printers. U.S. West has a deal with Liberate to deploy set-top boxes throughout its network and has already begun its first rollout in Minneapolis. Sony is producing an MP3 player as small as a fountain pen and the digital picture frame discussed earlier. And so on and so on.

The exciting thing is that once the fourth wave starts seeping its way into more and more areas of the economy, the industries it touches will begin to be influenced by the cost curve of the computer industry. This is because as music, or audio, or pictures, or what have you begin to be produced with bytes in mind, they're stored in a different form. Music is stored in zeros and ones (bits of data). Photographs are stored in pixels. Digital storage moves companies more in line with the computer industry cost curve, often referred to as Moore's law.

MORE ON MOORE

Moore was a bigwig at Intel. While there, he came up with a rule that basically said this: Every 18 months, the cost of computing is cut in half. In other words, every year and a half, for the same amount of money, customers can get twice the amount of computing.

Trace the cost of DRAM over a 20-year period, and you'll see what he means (see Figure 14.4). DRAM has gone down in price by 30 to 35 percent per year every year for the past 30 years. Compare this to the cost of cars or cereal, and you'll realize how outrageous it is. If these two items had followed the same cost curve from 1980 to 1998 as DRAM, a box of cereal would cost less than a penny and a car would cost about $25, instead of $20,000.

GOING INTO HYPERDRIVE

Have you ever tried to sip a thick shake through a thin straw? Frustrating, isn't it? Well, drinking a chocolate shake and downloading music might seem to have little in common, but they're more similar than you might think.

Right now, the average Web user is excitedly trying to suck superthick content (music, video, political scandal transcripts) through a superthin straw (a 56K modem hooked into a network of telephone wires), and it takes forever. Who wants to sit there for an hour and wait for an album to download when Tower Records is only a 10-minute drive away? For digital content to be compelling, it has to be delivered fast, and that means cable modems, T1 lines, or DSL connections.

FIGURE 14.4 CEREAL AND AUTOMOBILE PRICING CURVES VERSUS COMPUTER PRICE CURVE.

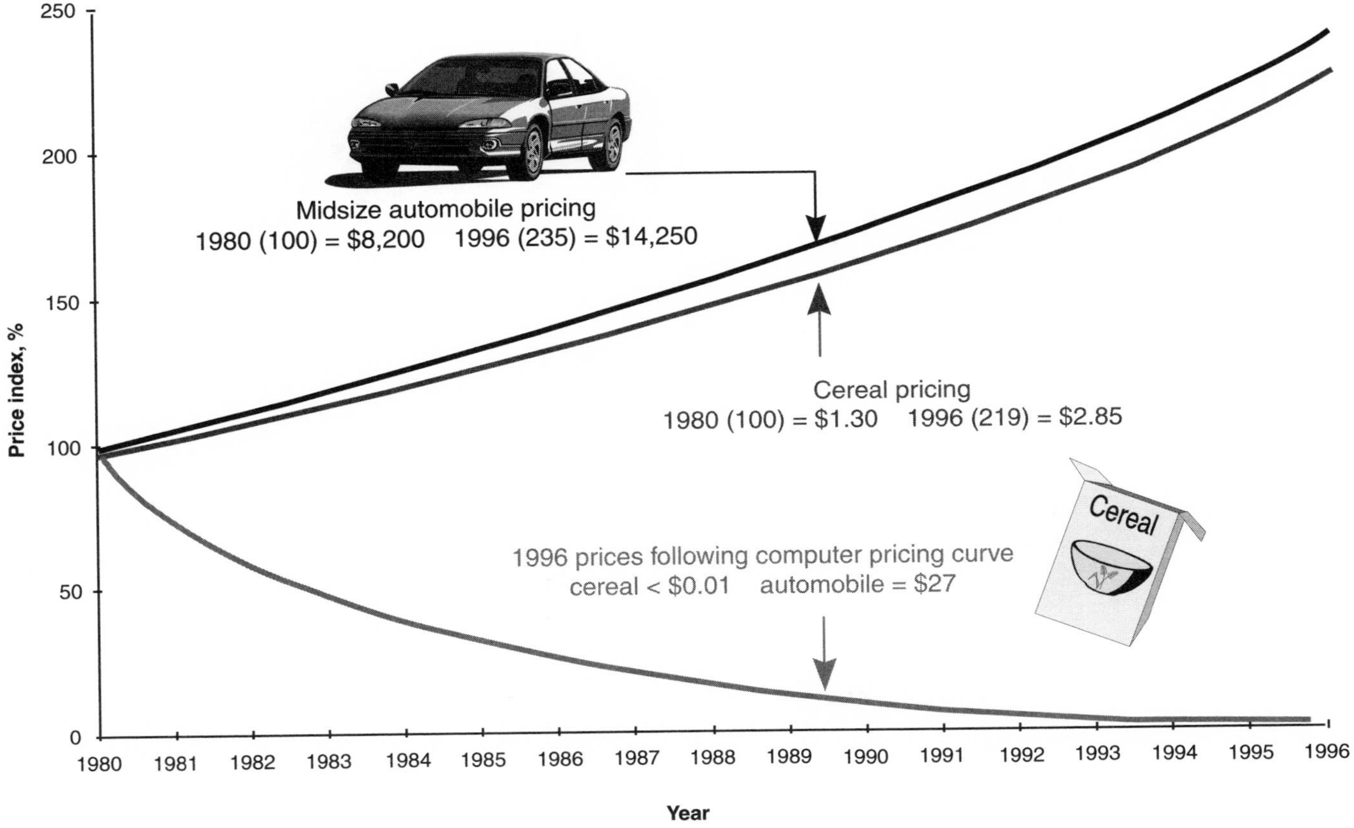

Midsize automobile pricing
1980 (100) = $8,200 1996 (235) = $14,250

Cereal pricing
1980 (100) = $1.30 1996 (219) = $2.85

1996 prices following computer pricing curve
cereal < $0.01 automobile = $27

Year

Price Index, %

Luckily, as these options become cheaper and more widely available, more and more people are bound to sign up. Already, a bandwidth explosion seems to be under way. Experts predict that by 2001, 10.5 million people will be connecting to the Web through a high-speed connection (see Figure 14.5).

PLACE YOUR BETS

Computers are going to be everywhere—from your car, to your television, to your refrigerator. It's obvious that many of these devices are going to share information, but *how* they will share it is less clear. The way that all of this eventually plays out will determine who the key companies of the next several decades will be—and who those key players are will determine how much their stock is worth.

If you're hip on investing in high tech, you need to consider who you think will take all of this technology to the next level—both the more obvious players (like Palm, Handspring, Research in Motion (RIM), and other companies that make handheld devices) and the less obvious (like EMC, a company that creates huge disk drives to store information digitally, plus the software

FIGURE 14.5   WORLDWIDE BROADBAND SUBSCRIBERS, MILLIONS.

	YEAR	
SYSTEM	1998	2001
Cable modem	0.7	5.2
DSL	0.1	4.5
Wireless	0.1	0.8
Total	0.9	10.5

Source: Dataquest and Michael Kwatinetz.

and services to make sure the content is always available). When you read about new developments in bandwidth, consider not only companies like AOL, which make compelling content, but companies like Cisco, which provide the infrastructure needed for any big bandwidth rollout.

In terms of fourth-wave players, the winners will be those who control content, or access to customers, or both. Audible was able to become a public company because it locked up the most spoken audio content available and put aggressive measures in place to ensure a large customer base. Nuvo Media, a leading provider of e-books, was not able to go public (and instead sold out to Gemstar) because it focused on the technology and didn't control content *or* customers.

Amazon could be a big winner in the fourth wave because it has the capability to introduce a large customer base to those controlling the content, but perhaps Barnes & Noble will acquire rights to all written book content for the Web and cut Amazon out of the loop. Who knows? No one. These are the kinds of issues you need to consider and the kinds of developments you need to follow. Technology is a slippery and ever-changing beast. Today's winners may be bankrupt tomorrow.

The key is to keep abreast of developments—and don't just *stand* there, test out the technology. Don't ever make the mistake of investing in something you do not understand. Surf the Web and download a book. Listen to some MP3 music files. Go to the store and try out any fourth-wave devices you can get your hands on. Check out a set-top box or a DSL connection. See what works and what doesn't, and form your own opinions about who will win this race into the future and who will be left in the dust.

SUMMING UP

The fourth wave will cause a dramatic shift in the way we live and how we use technology. It will cause major, currently low-tech, industries to be subsumed, including photography, music, books, brokerage, insurance, video, and more. Possible winners in the space include the following:

- Fourth-wave companies that control content and access to customers

- Infrastructure suppliers that provide bandwidth, storage, server technology, wireless communications, set-top boxes and more

- Device manufacturers that can tap into the market for taking fourth-wave content on the road

Epilogue

So there you have it. Class dismissed. All that remains is for you to start investing.

Over the course of this book I've thrown a lot of rules and measuring sticks your way. It may take awhile for you to turn those theories into practice. Be patient. The market rewards the informed investor.

Most of all, remember to think long term. The Dow and the NASDAQ can be finicky bedfellows. Many a pauper awakens one day to find himself a millionaire, but the reverse is also true. As I write this, in fact, Wall Street has experienced another tech wreck, and shares in some of technology's hottest companies are trading at an all-time low.

The good news is that you now have the tools you need to make turns like this one irrelevant. If you've done your homework, a market crash is nothing more than a fantastic opportunity to buy low.

Whatever the market is doing at any given time, keep your wits and confidence about you. Observe panic, but rise above it. And don't forget what you've learned in this book:

1. Concentrate your investments on a handful of companies.

2. Buy low, sell high.

3. Don't invest blindly.

4. Invest in great management.

5. Look for companies with a competitive advantage.

6. Love companies customers love.

7. Look for long-term thinkers.

8. Always look forward, not backward.

9. Pick only high-growth companies.

10. The best stocks are cheaper than you think.

Playing the stock market is like playing an instrument—practice makes perfect. Devote enough time each month to allow yourself to identify great companies, and to keep an eye on them. Don't get discouraged if a few of your picks don't do as well as you'd like—we all make mistakes. Besides, it only takes one superstar to make up for a handful of washouts.

Good luck. And happy hunting.

Index